Coming of Age in Africa

Through African Eyes: Cultures in Change

LEON E. CLARK, EDITOR

Coming of Age in Africa: Continuity and Change

EDITED BY
LEON E. CLARK

Unit I of THROUGH AFRICAN EYES: CULTURES IN CHANGE

FREDERICK A. PRAEGER, *Publishers*
New York • Washington • London

FREDERICK A. PRAEGER, *Publishers*
111 Fourth Avenue, New York, N.Y. 10003, U.S.A.
5, Cromwell Place, London S.W.7, England

Published in the United States of America in 1969
by Frederick A. Praeger, Inc., Publishers

Library of Congress Catalog Card Number: 72-89614

Printed in the United States of America

I call Gold,
Gold is mute.
I call Cloth,
Cloth is mute.
It is Mankind that matters.

Akan proverb (Ghana)

Contents

Preface and Acknowledgments

Through African Eyes has two main goals: to let Africans speak for themselves and to let students think for themselves.

The selections in this book come from a variety of sources, including autobiographies, speeches, case studies by social scientists, newspaper articles, novels, and poems. Almost all of them were written by Africans. Where an African source did not exist, or where it seemed more appropriate to have the view of an "outsider" (as in the section dealing with European colonial attitudes), the work of non-Africans was included. The aim throughout, however, is to capture African life as it is lived by the people, not as it is interpreted by observers.

This book differs from many other textbooks in social studies in that it does not "explain" Africa for you or tell you what you are supposed to think. Rather, it raises questions and points out problems, then provides materials for you to analyze in seeking the solutions. Sometimes there are no solutions; sometimes there are many answers to the same questions; sometimes the answers change as you discover new information.

More important than finding answers, however, is learning how to analyze problems. Today's solutions may be useless tomorrow, but the process of analysis will be even more important; it is our only way of making sense of new realities. This book, then, is geared for your future. It does not ask you simply to memorize facts, most of which you will forget anyway; it is designed to stretch your ability to think, an ability you will need for the rest of your life.

Thinking, of course, is only part of the total man; feeling is just as important, if not more so. The readings in this book are designed to help you *feel* what it is like to be African. Most of them are highly personal, first-hand accounts that draw you into the thoughts and emotions of individual people.

Africa as a continent may seem quite different from America, and it is, but Africans as people will probably strike you as being very similar to yourself. All human beings, after all, face the same needs: to eat, to work, to raise a family, to find entertainment, to get along with their fellow men. Learning how Africans manage their lives—sharing their experience—will help you to understand how people everywhere, including Americans, meet these basic needs.

*   *   *

Through African Eyes is the first product of the Educational Materials Project (EMPathy), which was established in June, 1967, for the express purpose of developing curricular materials for the study of other cultures. EMPathy is sponsored by the Conference on Asian Affairs, Inc., a nonprofit educational organization located in New York City, which works in close cooperation with the New York State Education Department.

The one man most responsible for the existence of EMPathy and hence for the development of the material represented by this book is Mr. Ward Morehouse, Director of the Center for International Programs and Comparative Studies, New York State Education Department. His unwavering support of the project has been a constant source of both personal and professional inspiration. His colleagues Dr. Arthur Osteen and Mr. Norman Abramowitz were also extremely helpful.

Special thanks should go to Miss Susan Hall, of Columbia University, for her invaluable research contributions to the first two units; to Mr. Kenneth Eisler, Professor Immanuel Wallerstein, of Columbia University, and Professor Edwin Fenton, of Carnegie-Mellon University, for their critical evaluation and editorial advice; and to my colleague Mr. Harlan Hamilton, of Jersey City State College, for his patience with the everyday problems of running an office.

For administrative support, I should also like to thank Dr. Howard Burnett, President of the College Center of the Finger Lakes, Corning, N. Y.

Finally, a special note of thanks should go to Mrs. Gladys Topkis, of Frederick A. Praeger, Inc. Without her quick understanding, sharp eye, and unlimited energy this book would never have survived the trauma of birth.

The editor, of course, bears ultimate responsibility for all the sins of omission and commission as regards the selection of material, the over-all approach to Africa, and the connective writing in the text.

The selections reprinted in this book originally appeared in the sources listed on the following page. Permission to reprint is gratefully acknowledged.

Luis Bernado Honwana, "The Hands of the Blacks," *New York Times Magazine,* April 30, 1967, pp. 26-27; trans. by Dorothy Guedes. © 1967 by The New York Times Company. Reprinted by permission of The New York Times Company and the Author.

Anna Apoko, "Growing Up in Acholi," in Lorene K. Fox, ed., *East African Childhood,* Nairobi, Kenya: Oxford University Press, 1967, pp. 45-47, 51-52, 53, 59-75.

Okot p'Bitek, *Song of Lawino,* Modern African Library, Nairobi, Kenya: East African Publishing House, 1966, pp. 16-17, 29, 32, 35, 41, 52-53, 59-60, 63, 65-67, 68-74, 77-79, 85-90, 95-97, 98-105.

Camara Laye, *Dark Child,* New York: Farrar, Straus & Giroux, 1954, pp. 11-12, 15-22, 141-47, 151-59; trans. by James Kirkup. Reprinted by permission of Farrar, Straus & Giroux and Wm. Collins Sons from *Dark Child,* copyright 1954 by Camara Laye.

Kwesi Brew, "Ancestral Faces," in John Reed and Clive Wake, eds., *A Book of African Verse,* London: Heinemann Educational Books, 1964, pp. 15-16. Reprinted by permission of the Publisher and the Author.

Ismael Hurreh, "Pardon Me," *Transition* Magazine, January, 1967, p. 36.

Léopold Sédar Senghor, "Totem," in Gerald Moore and Uilli Beier, eds., *Modern Poetry from Africa,* Baltimore: Penguin African Library, 1963, p. 46. Reprinted by permission of the Author.

LEON E. CLARK
Director, Educational Materials Project

Foreword: Through African Eyes

It seems appropriate—if not imperative—to have an African write the Foreword to this book. It is also important, of course, to have the Foreword relate to the central meaning of the book. The story "The Hands of the Blacks" answers both demands.

The author is Luis Bernado Honwana, a young journalist and short-story writer, who was born in a village in Mozambique, the Portuguese colony of East Africa. In 1966, at the age of 24, he was imprisoned by the Portuguese for "political subversive activities." "The Hands of the Blacks" appeared a year later, in *The New York Times*. The story presents only one episode in the life of a young African boy, but in a sense it summarizes the whole history of colonial Africa. And it goes beyond Africa to the experience of black men everywhere. Thus the story embodies the basic purpose of this book: to share with you the feelings, aspirations, and lives of black Africans and, even more, to help you to develop empathy—a feeling of identity—with your fellow man.

The Hands of the Blacks

by Luis Bernado Honwana

I don't remember now how we got onto the subject, but one day teacher said that the palms of the blacks' hands were much lighter than the rest of their bodies because only a few centuries ago they walked around on all fours, like wild animals, so their palms weren't exposed to the sun, which went on darkening the rest of their bodies. I thought of this when Senhor Padre told us after catechism that we were absolutely hopeless, and that even the blacks were better than we were, and he went back to this thing about their hands being lighter, saying that it was like that because they always went about with their hands folded together, praying in secret.

I thought this was so funny, this thing of the blacks' hands being lighter, that you should just see me now—I don't let go of anybody, whoever they are, until they tell me why they think that the palms of their hands are lighter. Dona Dores, for instance, told me that God made their hands lighter like that so they wouldn't dirty the food they made for their masters, or anything else they were ordered to do that should be kept quite clean.

Senhor Antunes, the Coca-Cola man, who only comes to the village now and again when all the cokes in the *cantinas* have been sold, said to me that everything I had been told was a lot of baloney. Of course I don't know if it was really, but he assured me it was. After I said yes, all right, it was baloney, then he told me what he knew about this thing of the blacks' hands. It was like this: "Long ago, many years ago, God, our Lord Jesus Christ, the Virgin Mary, St. Peter, many other saints, all the angels that were in heaven then, and some of the people who had died and gone to heaven— they all had a meeting and decided to make blacks. Do you know how? They got hold of some clay and pressed it into second-hand molds. And to bake the clay of the creatures they took them to the heavenly kilns. Because they were in a hurry and there was no room next to the fire, they hung them in the chimneys. Smoke, smoke, smoke—and there you have them, black as coals. And now do you want to know why their hands stayed white? Well, didn't they have to hold on while their clay baked?"

When he had told me this Senhor Antunas and the other men who were around us all burst out laughing, they were so pleased.

That very same day Senhor Frias called me after Senhor Antunes had gone away and told me that everything I had heard from them had been just one big pack of lies. Really and truly, what he knew about the blacks was right—that God finished making men and told them to bathe in a lake in heaven. After bathing the people were nice and white. The blacks, well, they were made very early in the morning, and at this hour the water in the lake was very cold, so they only wet the palms of their hands and the soles of their feet before dressing and coming into the world.

But I read in a book that happened to mention it that the blacks have hands lighter like this because they spent all their days bent over, gathering the white cotton in Virginia and I don't know where else. Of course, Dona Estefania didn't agree when I told her this. According to her, it's only because their hands became bleached with all that washing.

Well, I don't know what you'll think about all this, but the truth is that however callused and cracked they may be, a black's hands are always lighter than the rest of him. And that's that!

My mother is the only one who must be right about this question of a black's hands being lighter than the rest of his body. On the day that we were talking about this, we two, I was telling her what I already knew about the matter, and she couldn't stop laughing. What I found strange was that she didn't tell me at once what she thought about all this, and she only answered me when she was sure I wouldn't get tired of bothering her about it. And even then she was crying and clutching herself around the stomach as if she had laughed so much she couldn't bear it. What she said was more or less this:

"God made blacks because they had to be. They had to be, my son. He thought they really had to be. . . . Afterward, he regretted having made them because the other men laughed at them and took them off to their homes and put them to serve as slaves or not much better. But because He couldn't make them all turn white, for those who were used to seeing them black would complain, He made it so that the palms of their hands would be exactly like the palms of other men's hands. And do you know why that was? Of course you don't know, and it's not surprising, because many, many people don't know. Well, listen: it was to show that what men do is only the work of men . . . that what men do is done by hands that are the same—hands of people who, if they had sense, would know that before everything else they are men. He must have been thinking of this when He made it so that the hands of the blacks would be the same as the hands of all those men who thank God they're not black."

After telling me this, my mother kissed my hands.

As I ran off into the yard to play ball, I thought to myself that I had never seen her cry so much when nobody had even hit her or anything.

xvi

Coming of Age in Africa

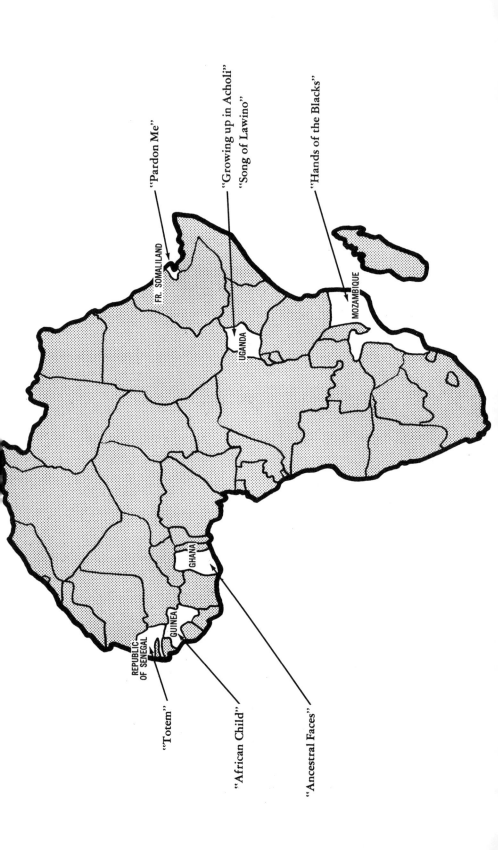

"Pardon Me"

"Growing up in Acholi"
"Song of Lawino"

"Hands of the Blacks"

FR. SOMALILAND

UGANDA

MOZAMBIQUE

REPUBLIC
OF SENEGAL

GUINEA

GHANA

"Totem"

"African Child"

"Ancestral Faces"

Introduction

Most Americans, when they think of Africa, imagine a jungle, huts, naked savages, and "backward" tribes. Some of these images are based on simple ignorance. For example, jungles make up only about one seventh of Africa; huts are almost impossible to find in the modern cities; and Africans—despite what Tarzan movies tell us—are no more savage than anyone else. In fact, they are much less savage than Europeans and Americans, if we judge people by the number of their fellow human beings they have killed in wars.

Ignorance, however, is only one reason for our misunderstanding of Africa; the other is our attitude. We tend to feel that people who do not live as we do must be backward. Our way, of course, is the *modern* way, sometimes called scientific or technological. Because our culture has excelled in making machines, for example, we tend to judge other people by the number of machines they have. We conveniently forget that Nazi Germany had very sophisticated machines. And we overlook the air pollution, water pollution, and general destruction of nature that our machines and factories have wrought, not to mention our possible destruction of all mankind through nuclear war. The hydrogen bomb may be the ultimate in war machinery, but dropping it might be considered the ultimate in human backwardness.

More important than our tendency to overlook our own

weaknesses, however, is our tendency to forget how unfair it is to use our own standards in judging other cultures. We apply *our* rules to someone else's game. This is like asking a football player to hit home runs. No matter how many touchdowns he scores, he will never measure up, because we are asking him to play by the rules of another game. This is obviously unfair. Many cultures, for example, feel that older people are very important, worthy of everyone's attention and respect. If these cultures were to judge us by looking at our old folks' homes—at how we try to get older people "out of the way"—they would say that we are savage and backward. From their point of view, of course, we are. But there are reasons for the way we behave, just as there are reasons for the way everyone behaves. We can understand other people only if we find out *why* they behave as they do. In short, cultures should be judged only from the inside. In a sense, we have to ask people what game they are playing; only then will we know what rules to apply.

Every child, almost from the moment of birth, begins to learn the rules of his culture's game. "Eat with your fork," "Say thank you," "Stand up when a lady enters the room," and so forth. Such rules—and hundreds more like them, some conscious and some unconscious—have to be learned before we know how to behave in society. The process by which we learn these rules is called *socialization.* Those who *socialize* us, of course, are the adults in society, particularly our parents.

The material in this unit deals with the process of growing up in Africa. It gives us an inside view of how African children are socialized, how they learn the rules of their culture. Therefore it should give us a basic understanding of why Africans behave the way they do—from an African point of view.

Of course, not all Africans are alike; there are literally hundreds of different societies on the African continent, each with its own culture and set of rules. But all African cultures have one thing in common: they are basically traditional, even though they are changing. The word "traditional" has a very special meaning when applied to cultures, and it usually refers to Africa, Asia, and Latin America—about two thirds of the world. In contrast, the cultures of Europe and North America are usually called *modern.*

Traditional cultures have a number of characteristics in common. For example, they all tend to be non-scientific and non-industrial. Their members tend to work in the fields rather than in factories, living a life close to nature. They also tend to emphasize a spiritual rather than a scientific control of nature, and their art is related very closely to God. For our purposes, however, it is important to concentrate on the family structure of traditional societies.

In the West, when we think of the family, we usually think of our immediate family: mother, father, and children. Sociologists call this group the *nuclear family.* The rest of the family falls into the category of relatives. Uncles, aunts, cousins, and even grandparents lie outside the nuclear family. A diagram of our family structure might look something like this:

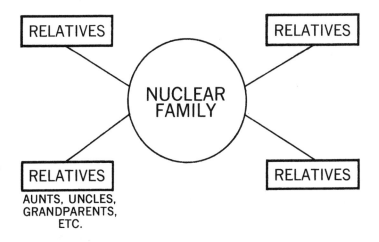

In traditional societies, however, the family is much different. The immediate family is not limited to the nuclear family;

rather, it includes all the people we in a modern society call relatives, such as aunts, uncles, and cousins. This larger immediate family is called the *extended family*. In this system, uncles and aunts have almost as much authority over children as the "real" parents, and cousins are regarded as brothers and sisters. Grandparents are looked up to as the parents of the whole group.

The relationships in traditional societies do not stop here. Often several extended families live together in a village, tracing their heritage to a common ancestor. Thus they form another group, called a *clan*. And a collection of clans makes a tribe. A diagram of traditional African relationships, then, might look something like this:

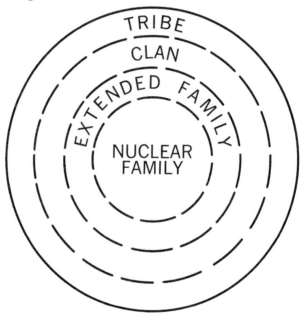

As you might expect, the "group" is extremely important in African society. As a result, people are seldom alone. In the West, on the other hand, we emphasize the individual. As a result we have much more privacy. Some Westerners feel, however, that we have too much privacy, creating such problems as loneliness, boredom, and alienation (a sense of being cut off from other people). The hippies, for example, go so far as to say we ought to retribalize.

This may or may not be a good idea. But it does point up an important fact: no society is perfect, even in its own terms; a society can always improve. Just as Africa can learn from the West, so we can, perhaps, learn from Africa. If nothing else, our attempt to understand African societies will help us to understand all societies, including our own.

Growing Up in Acholi

by Anna Apoko

PART I

[Tribes in Africa, like groups everywhere in the world, are held together by common interests. Each tribe has its own customs, beliefs, rituals, and, in some cases, its own language and dress. No two tribes are quite the same; each tribe is something "special." Traditionally, every African is born into a tribe, marries a member of the same tribe, and passes on these "special" customs to the next generation. Today Africa is changing rapidly, but the tribal system still lies at the base of African life.

There are more than 800 tribes in Africa, and they range in size from a mere 200 to more than 20 million members. You are about to read a first-hand account of what it is like to grow up in one of these tribes, the Acholi of northern Uganda, in East Africa. The Acholi tribe today has approximately 250,000 members. The author, an Acholi herself, wrote this description while she was a college student, in 1966.

As you read Part I, think of these questions:

What groups exist within the Acholi tribe? What are the purposes of these groups?

How do the Acholi pass on their traditions to their children? (In other words, how are the children socialized?)

Who are the teachers in Acholi society?

What are the important values of the Acholi? What are the characteristics of the ideal Acholi man? The ideal woman?]

THE VILLAGE

. . . The Acholi people were originally divided into several chiefdoms. The most important of these were Payira, Patiko, Puranga, and Koich, my own chiefdom, with which I am mainly concerned. Each chiefdom has many clans and each clan has many families. Groups of families, who are very often related to one another, live together in a village. The population of a village often drinks from the same well, and groups all the crops in the same place every year. A village with many people can also have a dancing field, with a high pole in the center for the drum. (Acholi dancers have been famous throughout Uganda for many years.)

People living in the same village have a lot in common. When the rainy season approaches, the men often go together to open one another's new cotton, simsim [a seed from which cooking oil is made], groundnut, or millet fields in turn. This makes digging easier and more enjoyable than if one man tries to work alone on his field. The man whose new cotton field is to be opened always arranges a beer party for the workers. The women also work in groups, helping one another weed in their gardens.

Within each village family in Acholi, there is a strict division of labor between the father and the mother, or husband and wife. The father or husband is the head of the family. He has the decisive voice on all matters concerning

9

Young Acholi girls (top) learn the role of women, while boys and men (below) perform a task restricted to men only. (Photos above by Paula Foster; photo below by Herman Schlenker, courtesy International Film Foundation)

the family. Acholi people follow the patrilineal system of inheritance [handing down wealth from father to son only]. Every father makes it a point to train his son to become a strong-willed man who cannot be dominated by a woman. The husband's work is the cutting of wood for building a house and the actual building of the house.

The wife's work is to cut grass for thatching the roof. The man also digs the field and sows the seed, but it is the work of the woman to keep the garden clear of weeds and to harvest the crops. . . . All domestic work concerned with cooking is the work of the woman. It is a disgrace for a grown-up man or even a boy to go to the well and carry water. That is the work of a woman. Grinding is also the work of a woman; no man in Acholi must grind. Anything concerned with babies and young children is woman's work.

A man who has so many acres of cotton, millet, and simsim, so many grain stores full of millet, simsim, and peas, who has so many cows or goats; a man whose houses are big and strong; a man who is brave in hunting and fighting— is considered a good and successful man in rural Acholi and is respected by society. A lot of songs are often composed, especially by women, for such men. For example, this one:

> *Odai we ye,*
> *Odai latin acel pire tek,*
> *Obutu kicel long gang oling tik.*

> Our Odai,
> The only great one.
> He was absent for a day
> and the house went to pieces.

11

Likewise, a woman whose house is well smeared with black soil and kept clean; who has a lot of food in her home; who cooks and gives generously to visitors [according to Acholi custom which requires the wife to give food to any visitor, whenever he comes]; a woman whose gardens are well kept; who mixes freely and happily with other women in the village; and who has children—is considered a good woman. Such a woman can be called to join a meeting of village elders to give some talks and advice. Very often such things as this are said about her: *Dako pa Okot dako ki cumun. Dako man minne opwongo ada.* ("Mrs. Okot is a woman and a half. She must have had really good training from her mother.")

Such are the Acholi's ideal people, those who are liked and valued by the whole community. The aim of traditional education or of bringing up children in Acholi is to produce such citizens. People take great care to see that children are given all the necessary training in order that they will be hard-working and useful men and women in the society; men and women who will not have to starve because they cannot cultivate for themselves. Great attention is paid to all aspects of children's "moral" development. They must learn to obey those who are older than they are. A boy, particularly, has to grow up obeying his father's brothers, who are just as important and influential to him as his own father. He must respect his mother's brothers, who may curse him and cause ill luck for him if he disrespects them. He must also grow up in close contact with the gods of his grandfathers and must know how to keep *abila,* the shrine.

Everybody who is closely related to the child takes part in and contributes toward the child's education. Uncles, aunts, stepmothers, elder brothers and sisters, all are members of staff. Teaching takes place through teasing (*ngala*), songs, educative stories (*ododo*), and practical work.

*   *   *

THE FEEDING AND CARE OF CHILDREN

... As soon as a mother has given birth to her baby, if she does not have older children of her own, she looks around among her relatives for *lapidi,* a selected young child, preferably a girl from six to ten years old, to act as the baby's "nurse." During my recent vacation I met a woman who was once my classmate; she had come sixty-five miles from where she was living with her husband, back to her father's home, looking for *lapidi.* She found a little girl, five years old, who went back with her.

The very young baby, from one to three months old, is tied on *lapidi*'s back. *Lapidi,* carrying the baby this way, goes with the mother to the field where she may be working most of the day. If the baby wakes up from his sleep and begins to cry, the mother unties it from the child's back and feeds it. By the time the baby is four months old, it may be left at home with *lapidi,* who again follows after the mother as soon as the baby is hungry and begins to cry. Nurses have many lullaby songs which they sing when the babies cry. For example, this:

> *Latin kok ngo?*
> *Meni otedo aluri ki kwon.*

> Baby, why do you cry?
> Your mother has cooked a fowl and some millet.

13

Sometimes the nurse becomes so tired, poor child, that she may begin wearily singing a song about the mother of the child, such as: *Min latin do tedo dyerwor . . .:* "The child's mother cooks so late in the night." If the mother has the food nearly ready she calls, "Bring me my baby! Do not break its back!" But when . . . she has not yet cooked the millet, she will say to *lapidi*, "Take the baby and play with it, out of my sight!" If the baby goes on crying, the nurse will again tie it on her back and follow the mother about the house.

Girls learn how to care for babies at an early age by serving as lapidis. *(Photo by Herman Schlenker, courtesy International Film Foundation)*

I was *lapidi* for my little cousin for about a year. How I loved that baby! I wanted to be with him all the time. Perhaps this was because I had requested to be *lapidi*. The duty had not been forced on me. By the time the baby was able to walk well and firmly and another little girl cousin was old enough to be nurse, I had to give him up so that I could go to school.

14

A mother who does not have *lapidi* is bound to carry her baby about wherever she goes and whatever she does. Such mothers often sing this lullaby to their babies:

> *Nynyu ka ikok ngo?*
> *Lapidi meri peke.*
> *Onyu ling,*
> *Lapidi meri obeno.*
>
> Why do you cry, my baby?
> You have no *lapidi?*
> *Obeno* is your nurse.
> Keep quiet, baby, you have no nurse.

Thus *lapidi* is second mother to the baby; and there are some babies who are fonder of their *lapidi* than of their own mothers.

*   *   *

GROWING FROM PLAY INTO WORK ACTIVITIES

After weaning [when he begins to eat solid food], the child sees less of his mother and more of his nurse, whose job is now to keep him company and to play with him. Very often the nurse, with the child on her hip or back, will join the company of other nurses and children. Together they form a play group. A large part of the day may be spent by the nurse in this group play while the mother and father of the baby are at work in the home or the field. . . . When the mother has to be away from the house, she will leave cooked food for the children and tell the nurse where to find it.

Toys are few among Acholi village children. Commercial toys, like dolls, ducks, building bricks, little motor cars, are

15

not given to Acholi children, except in the relatively few homes in which parents have had a school education and can afford to buy them. Most children are responsible for finding their own play materials. Almost anything can be made into a useful toy by children. Leaves, old tins, corncobs, broken pieces of pottery, fruit, seeds, anything they can pick up will be used by the children as toys. This constant eagerness for toys, on the part of the younger children in particular, often leads to the destruction of valuable possessions of the family. Finding at home such fascinating objects as ballpoint pens, for example, or even the grown-ups' shoes, young children, having little else to play with and not being allowed to wander about very far, will often put such objects to use in their play. They may afterwards leave them thrown around in the courtyard. Parents, upon finding them perhaps in bad condition, may punish the children severely.

Acholi children spend much of their time playing out to their satisfaction the roles of adults. Little girls can often be found playing the part of their mothers. They pick up corncobs, sticks, or bottles, pretending that these are their babies. Sometimes they will sit on the ground, stretching their legs out straight and holding the little "babies" on their laps. . . . They will pick up little stones, in place of millet, and start grinding them on the sand. Then, putting together three little stones, they will pretend to make the fire. Old tins and broken pieces of pots are their cooking utensils.

Young boys, already aware of the work of their sex, often like to pull grasses and build little huts. They model motor cars and lorries [trucks] out of clay. Sometimes they will break off a branch full of leaves, perhaps a big branch, which they use for a motor car. With two or three children astride, they "drive" rapidly along the ground. Young children want to be active. They like running informal races on their own, climbing trees, singing and dancing. There is no strict grouping of boys and girls in these earlier years. Much of the time they will be seen, and heard, playing together.

A growing number of village children of six to ten now go to primary school. There are still some, however, who do not go, either because their parents cannot afford or do not want to send them to school or because the nearest school is four or five miles away, too far for a young child to walk every day. In the latter case, the children may start school when they are older. By this time boys and girls usually stay strictly in their own groups. The separation is encouraged by parents, especially mothers, who feel that it is not proper for their daughters to play among boys. The children themselves have abusive songs which they sing to a child of the opposite sex who may try to join their group. *Labed, kin litino co!* "The girl who stays among boys," they will sing, or vice versa. Such songs will usually force the child to leave that company and join the proper one. . . .

At mealtime all the children eat with the mother, sitting on the kitchen floor, while the father eats alone. It is common in the villages to find a group of two or three families eating together, each woman having cooked two separate dishes, one for the men and one for the women and children. If there is a large number of children, one separate dish may be served to the children only. The two or three men, heads of different families, will sit near a fire outside or inside a house. They put each woman's dish in their midst and eat them in turn.

It is considered very important that when children are eating, they sit up straight, without supporting themselves

17

on the arm. This leaning on the arm is considered a sign of laziness in the child, and mothers cannot tolerate it. Most mothers want their children to eat quickly, taking big mouthfuls of food. They do not want them to take a long time, eating so slowly that the food is finished by other people before they, the children, are satisfied. This, most women think, tempts the children to go back to the cooking pot to steal more food. Again, children are made to keep quiet when they are eating. "You haven't got two mouths," they are told, "that you can eat with one and talk with the other." . . .

For the girls of primary-school age, their time of playing is nearly over. Home training and stricter discipline begin. At this age the girls must stop eating chicken or any kind of fowl. (An Acholi woman does not eat any part of a fowl.) The child now has real duties to perform. If she has younger sisters or brothers, she will be a nurse. If she does not have a younger child to look after, and in some cases even if she does, the little girl is expected to make two or three journeys to the well, carrying a small container on her head in which to fetch water. She may be told by her mother who is cooking beans or meat to keep the fire burning. It may be her job also to look after the millet and peas spread out in the sun to dry, keeping the chickens away, collecting and putting the food in the house if it rains. A girl of eight or nine may be expected to grind millet or simsim with her mother, or to accompany her mother into the field to help dig. If her father is away at mealtime, the little girl may be asked to take the responsibility of cooking for him, having the food ready by the time he gets back. There is a dual purpose for this thorough training of the girl. It is partly to prepare her for her future duties as a housewife and a mother, and partly to help the mother, who, in the Acholi village, has many pressing jobs to do.

The girls who go to school, of course, have much less time for doing any household chores. Many girls have to leave their homes at seven in the morning, returning as late as half-past seven in the evening. . . . If the school is several miles distant, they cannot come home for lunch. Thus they have little time to practice cooking and other household duties. But some Acholi parents still reserve certain tasks which their primary-school girls must perform anyway.

Since most of the secondary schools are boarding schools, the older girls who attend them are away from their homes for a full nine months of the year and so are out of reach of further traditional training by their mothers. For this reason schools are often considered by Acholi parents as making their daughters lazy.

There is conflict between the schoolgirls and their mothers when they do return home. At school, the girls are taught to be clean and smart, with heavy school assignments but little if any manual work to be done. When they come home, they resent having to spend the whole day in the hot sun, weeding in the fields with their hands. They dislike having to grind large amounts of millet on the grinding stone. How can they keep clean and smart, they ask, with all these dirty jobs to do? Further, the fact that most of their schools are mixed schools makes many Acholi mothers reluctant to send their daughters to school. They fear that by mixing so much with boys, by learning and speaking English all the time, and by having no practice in traditional manners and housekeeping, the girls are likely to become *malaya* (prostitutes) in the towns. This is one of the reasons why the education of women in Acholi has tended to lag behind.

The boys, on the other hand, are freer from adult attention until a much later age. From the age of five years, after the separation from the girls, the boys usually play in a gang. They play much wilder games now, too. Shooting or trapping birds is one of their favorite pastimes. They make for themselves *abutidda* [slingshots], small Y-shaped twigs of a tree with rubber strings attached. With these they shoot stones at birds, often going as far as a mile or so from home to hunt. This takes much of their time. Almost every day, too, they will go in a group to the river to wash their bodies and take a swim.

Another favorite game for Acholi boys at this age is *cobo lawala*. A *lawala* is a willow, bent and tied like a ring about one foot in diameter. Each boy cuts himself a beautiful thin stick about six feet long to use as a spear. The gang divides into two teams. A boy from one team will throw the *lawala* spinning through the air to the other team with all his might; then all of the boys in that team, standing in line, will try to thrust their spears into the center of the ring. So long as one boy in the team succeeds in spearing and bringing down the *lawala,* the other team will keep throwing it for them to spear. A boy who is expert at *lawala* is always very good at hunting too. He will seldom miss the running animal when he goes hunting. Because boys who go to school do not have all the time required for practicing *lawala,* they can never hope to be really good hunters with spears. As more and more of the Acholi boys now go to school, the game of *lawala* is gradually dying out.

Growing Up in Acholi

[In Part I we saw that the ideal Acholi male is strong and brave, a decisive family leader, a builder, and a farmer. The ideal female is generous, happy, obedient, a bearer of children, and a good housekeeper. In some ways these ideals are similar to American ideals; in other ways they are different.

Such "ideal types," as sociologists call them, do not exist in reality, of course, because no one ever becomes perfect. But they do exist in the minds of people, in the collective mind of society. They stand as goals to reach for and as standards against which we can test our behavior. As such they have a profound effect on our lives.

On the most obvious level, of course, ideal types determine what we are allowed or supposed to do. Acholi men may build a house but may not carry water; the women may care for children but may not go hunting. In more subtle ways, ideal types determine the kinds of experiences people have, particularly while growing up. American boys, for example, may not play with dolls after a certain age, just as Acholi girls may not play hunting games. In short, ideal types stand behind all the do's and don't's presented to men and women.

As we saw in Part I, the total process of learning how to

behave is called socialization. It is society's way of making people conform to its ideals. These ideals, or values, vary from society to society, and therefore the details of socialization also vary; but, regardless of its ideals, every society engages in socialization. If it did not, it would not be a society; it would not have a common set of values that bind people together.

Since a society begins with values and then socializes its members according to these values, we can find out the values of any society by examining its process of socialization, the way it passes its rules on to the young. By working backwards, so to speak, we can infer the values that lie behind the process. By examining the lullabies that are sung, the games that are played, and the experiences that are created at home and at school, we can discover what a society considers to be right and good.

As you read Part II, think of these questions:

How are teenage girls in Acholi treated in comparison to boys?

What does this treatment tell you about the ideal types in Acholi society?

Why are roles important in society?

How do Acholi parents compare with American parents?]

ACHOLI PARENTS AS TEACHERS

Children's relationships with their parents depend, first of all, on the ages of the children. Young babies are very close to their mothers or nurses. Most fathers in Acholi do not have a close relationship with babies. It is a woman's job to look after them. . . . Moreover, Acholi men spend most of the day away from their homes. After digging in the morning, they eat their meal and then go off to visit their friends or attend beer parties.

After weaning, even the mother-child relationship breaks considerably. The child now spends most of his time with the nurse. If the mother has no nurse, she may take her child to join some other group of children, where she will leave him to play until she returns. This happens when the child has become too heavy to carry about, or the mother has another baby to take his place. Sometimes, such children are taken to their grandmother's to be looked after. There is a tendency, however, for grandparents to spoil children by overfeeding and perhaps carrying them on their backs even if they are too heavy. For this reason, mothers hesitate to send their children to spend long periods with their grandparents.

Child-parent relationships also depend on the sex of the child. After weaning, boys do not have a close relationship with their mothers anymore. From two to six years old, a boy spends most of his time with a nurse and then with a gang of other boys. When a boy is about eight years old he can accompany his father to the garden to dig, although very often he is excused to come home earlier than his father. His mother will give him food, and, after eating, off he goes to play. In the early evenings he may go with his father for a walk around the fields or into the jungle to collect some logs. These logs are burned in the courtyard fire which the family gathers around in the evening. The boy is usually told to sweep the compound before he lights the evening fire.

When he grows a little older, the father will show him the total area of his field, where it starts and where it ends, so that in future nobody can take it from him. During their walks in the evening, father and son carry spears. A father

23

will tell his son to carry a spear or two whenever he goes into the jungle, in case an animal or an enemy appears. He tells the young boy all he knows about the behavior of certain dangerous animals, and what to do when they appear. He shows him which trees are good, or bad, for building houses or grain stores, for making a hoe, and so on. Gradually, as the boy grows older, he is able to fetch the logs and make the fire without being told or helped.

The expansion of school education, and especially of boarding schools, has seriously weakened this father-son relationship. Day school boys do come home in the evening, when they are expected to sweep the compound and light the evening fire. In the evening the boy sits outside by the fire with his father while the mother is still preparing supper.

The girls, on the other hand, spend more time with their mothers from the beginning. Almost as soon as the girl passes the breast-feeding stage, she is given little jobs to do. She goes to the garden with her mother, perhaps helping or pretending to help with a very small hoe. She also goes with her mother to fetch firewood. Acholi mothers pay great attention to the development of their little daughters. If even the young child shows a tendency toward being lazy in doing these small home duties, the mother may become very worried about her. She may even beat the girl for it. (I remember my own mother slapping me on the face because at ten years of age I had not learned to grind millet well.) In the late evening, when father and brother are out sitting by the fire, the little girl stays inside, helping her mother get the food ready. Again, girls who go to school have less time with their mothers. They are therefore considered lazy and inefficient houseworkers by traditional Acholi standards.

. . . It is the concern of all the relatives, not only the

parents, to bring up the child properly and make him fit into and be useful in the village community. It is, therefore, a duty of the growing child to obey all his relatives. He is strictly taught by his parents to say nothing rude to anybody, including relatives. A little girl can be asked by any woman in the village to grind some millet, fetch some water, or cook something for her. Any male relative can request a little boy to run an errand or help him in some other way. Children are expected to do all these things without complaining. Those who do not obey will always have a bad reputation in the village. They are often told the proverb *Lalek camo wi ogwang mutwo*: "The child who cannot do any favor for people eats the bony skull of a wildcat." Or the proverb *Okwero pwony cito ki cet pa maro:* "If you do not listen to people's advice, you will go mannerless to your mother-in-law's home." This would be a disgrace, of course. The place where every man or woman should show the best behavior is in a mother-in-law's house.

DISCIPLINE IN TRIBAL EDUCATION

There is a constant attempt on the part of the adults, then, to mold the character and behavior of children. A child who talks too much or asks too many questions is discouraged by adults from so doing. A child who cries often without a real cause is whipped by the father, mother, or a relative until he keeps quiet.

The girls from the earliest years tend to be more disciplined and restricted than the boys. . . . Mothers are very particular about the way in which little girls sit. From one and a half years onward, the girl is repeatedly told and

25

warned to sit down smartly with her knees together. If even a small girl sits carelessly, she may be whipped by the mother. I have twin nieces, aged two and a half, who are already so particular about their sitting habits that they keep reminding each other to sit properly. They often tell the adults to see how well they sit.

Another strict rule for the girls is that they should keep close to the homestead. No mother wants her four- to six-year-old daughter wandering from home to home. This is considered a very bad and dangerous practice, which may lead to poisoning or to future prostitution of the girl. Nevertheless, a group of girls are permitted to go together to the well or to fetch firewood.

Girls also have to obey their big brothers, who have authority over their younger siblings. A fifteen-year-old boy may order his sister to cook quickly for him because he is in a hurry to go to a dance. He may order her to clean his house or fetch him some water for washing his clothes. The girl must respond to these orders with perfect obedience. Failure to do so often leads to a fight between the two children, almost always to the disadvantage of the girl, who may be the smaller or physically weaker of the two. Parents tend to ignore or even encourage these incidents, since the role of the Acholi female is to be obedient. "You will suffer great blows from somebody's son if you do not practice obedience now," the girls are often told.

Older brothers are also very particular about the way their grown-up sisters behave in the presence of their boyfriends. If a boy sees his sister misbehaving in any way, he is authorized by his parents to give her a good beating. The sisters are very important to the brothers, whose future can largely depend on them. A brother whose sister has good manners and is married is sure to have a wife himself. . . . Since he cannot marry until his sister is married, it is his real concern to see that she is well behaved enough to be married early.

Acholi parents do not like their children to steal things. If even a young child shows a tendency toward stealing, he is severely punished by beating; he may be denied his meals for a whole day, or until he confesses and promises to steal no more.

THE ADOLESCENT YEARS

From the age of fifteen onward, children are treated in a much more respectful manner. Everybody in the village accepts the fact that the child *odoko dano,* has become a person. No mother wants to beat her daughter at this age. It would be considered a shameful disgrace. If the girl does anything wrong, the mother corrects her in words only, or she may refer her to an aunt or some older relative who will give her advice.

By this time an Acholi village girl is highly accomplished by traditional standards. She does most of the cooking in the home now, doing everything without being told. She knows, or ought to know, exactly what her duties are. A mother with a grown-up girl is very lucky. For almost the first time, the Acholi mother can go and relax with her friends, knowing that the daughter is performing the household duties well in her absence. When the mother is at home, she can sit and instruct the girl as she works. No good girl can sit and do nothing while her mother is working. This could give her a bad reputation which would make her marriage difficult. There are many songs composed to warn such girls:

27

Min anyaka too ka rego
Colo nyaka pe
Nyako obedo kilao
Min anayaka too yo kulu
Calo nyaka pet
Nyako obedo kilao

The mother of the girl
Suffers all the way
Going to the well
Grinding and so on
As if she has no daughter to help her.
This girl is hopeless.

The Acholi girls at this stage, educated or not, are usually very particular about cleanliness, of their bodies and of the house. On entering any home in the village, one can tell from the appearance of the house whether there is an adolescent girl in the family. A house where there is such a girl is usually kept constantly and smartly smeared with black soil. Along the wall, the girl will hang rows of clean white calabashes, very cleverly decorated. Some have *adungu,* a musical instrument played by girls, hung up there too. Outside, somewhere behind the house, one sees a heap of firewood, neatly tied into bundles. These are the signs of the presence of a wonderful girl in the home. . . .

The adolescent boy is treated respectfully, too. The presence of an adolescent boy, or boys, in the home is indicated by an extra house, or houses, in the compound, the bachelor huts. Each grown-up boy is entitled to a hut of his own. He is highly respected by his mother, who keeps a separate dish for him whenever she cooks. Each year, the boy must, by himself or with the help of his father, open an acre of cotton for his own use. My brother, who is sixteen, has got the first acre of cotton to which he is entitled.

Boys of this age spend a lot of their time away from the home. Nobody minds where they go or at what time of night they come back to their huts. At this age it is considered normal and proper for a boy to go out looking for a wife. Any father would be worried and suspect that something was wrong with his son if he did not show these signs. In case of any misconduct by the boy—for example, if he gets a girl into trouble—the father always pays the necessary fine for it, and does so without much complaint. The mother, contrary to what one would suppose, tends to be happy when her son does this. She expects, and it does happen, that the girl who is in trouble will soon come and spend a few months with her until the illegal baby is delivered. During her stay with the boy's family, she will relieve his mother of her household duties. This is a time of trial for the girl, however. Just like a student teacher on teaching practice, she must show her talents if she hopes to get married into the family, and the whole society approves of this. The result is that such girls tend to be overworked in the boy's, or what turns out to be the mother-in-law's, home.

Growing Up in Acholi

PART III

[Thus far in our reading we have examined the traditional way of life of the Acholi. We have seen how male and female roles are sharply distinguished; we have seen how these roles are based on clearly defined ideal types that have been passed on from generation to generation; and, finally, we have seen how the process of socialization attempts to perpetuate this traditional way of life—how parents serve as teachers, how discipline is applied, and how children and adolescents are treated.

All societies, of course, attempt to perpetuate themselves by socializing their young. Parents, after all, want their children to be like them, at least to share the same values and general approach to life. But change does take place, even when the older generation fights against it. Time brings new conditions to the world, and societies must make new adjustments if they are to survive.

Change, however, even though it is inevitable, usually takes place gradually, especially change in social practices. To change the roles of men and women, for example, a society must establish new ideal types and then alter its process of socialization. All this takes time. (Consider how long it has taken women to gain "equality" in America, and it is still almost unthinkable to have a woman president.)

In this assignment you will read about some of the changes taking place in Acholi. Try to keep in mind the traditional way of life as a point of contrast, particularly the traditional roles of men and women and the process of socialization.

As you read Part III, think of these questions:

What changes are taking place in Acholi? Which do you consider good? Which bad?

What is causing these changes?

Which members of the Acholi favor these changes? Which do not? Why not?

How do these changes compare with changes taking place in America today?]

POSTSCRIPT

In Acholi today there are hundreds of families who live exactly as I have explained above. This includes most of the people in my own clan, although changes are beginning to affect them also. Our old clan forest, beginning several miles outside of Gulu, extends for twenty-eight miles. Many family farms are included in this stretch, a few of them very progressive. My father's farm is one of these. We raise cotton, millet, maize, simsim, cassava, groundnuts, and all our own fruit and garden vegetables. My four sisters and I, my brother, my late mother, my present stepmother, my father, and some of his brothers, all worked in the fields when I was growing up.

We still love farm life. My sister, who has just returned from almost two years of infant teacher training in England, tells us how she used to miss the work in the fields, especially during the long vacations. Her British friends could hardly believe that this was true. I myself, when I was home for the recent Easter break from Makerere College, sowed our entire groundnut crop and was proud to do it. Now, several months later, the groundnuts have matured and are ready to be harvested. My sister, my cousins, or my father perhaps will pull the groundnut plants in my absence, leaving them in the field to dry in the sun. We can do this because, as my sister remarked, the population of our area are still good people. There is no stealing yet.

It is sad to think that only as civilization comes to Acholi communities are the people beginning to steal, so that farmers soon will not be able to leave their groundnuts or maize or other crops safely in the fields to dry.

For this is a period of rapid development in East Africa. The old economic and social structure is disintegrating in many ways. Gradually it is being replaced by a money economy. There are Acholi farmers who go from the village now to earn money in the towns. Some of these men leave their wives in the village, there to produce food for their families, while the men work for money in the towns. When they earn what they feel is enough, these farmers come back to the village.

Some of the younger men, who, having received some primary or junior secondary education, find work in the towns, may take their wives and young children with them. They are able to buy more or less permanent homes on the outskirts, or to rent houses provided in quarters or housing estates inside the towns. This class of men is increasing rapidly in Acholi. Most of them work as clerks, office messengers, and such. They are joined by the growing number of teachers, better educated, who also leave their homes or villages to teach in whatever schools they are assigned to. In this class of people, the men or women will earn money, and that is all. Their farming or food production is limited to small vegetable gardens. Most of the family food is bought at the market. . . .

A few other changes affecting the care of Acholi children should be mentioned. Take eating practices. The custom by which several families have their meals together is restricted to villages now, where it is still quite common, especially among the uneducated or less-educated families. Village families which go to the towns will usually eat their own food. It is still common practice, however, even in the towns, for the children to be given their meals separately. Many town wives eat separately, too, their working men unable to come home for food in the middle of the day. The men are often too late returning home in the evening for their wives and the children to wait. There are some Acholi families, especially the families of teachers, where husband and wife eat together at a table.

Sleeping facilities for children are improving. In most educated Acholi homes now, babies and other children have beds of their own. Most working men living in town have proper beds for their children as well as for themselves. In a very few advanced homes, the mothers have prams in which the babies can be pushed and can sleep. It is usually only when these families come back to visit their village relatives that the mats are again spread on the floor for sleeping.

Many of these improvements are coming about because of the changing attitudes of Acholi villagers toward school education. The Uganda Ministry of Education figures for June, 1965, indicate that 80 percent of the school-age children in Acholi attend government schools. Even in the

33

villages, the number is growing rapidly. This has been a tremendous development, bringing improvements in many aspects of living. In the primary school, for example, all children are given health training. They are taught to wash their bodies every day, to keep their nails and hair short, to brush their teeth. And to make sure that they do all this, some teachers require that the children do it in school every day. This is bound to have a good effect on the school-age children. . . .

More and more African girls are going to school. These young Tanzanians are learning simple crafts to teach to village women. (Photo by George Holton, courtesy UNICEF)

The changing attitudes of Acholi villagers toward the school education of girls is especially important. So often I think how well my elder sisters would have done in life if they had been given opportunities for education similar to mine. In their childhood, though, . . . it was almost unthinkable for girls to be sent to school. I remember that even in my junior secondary-school days, a group of us were taken with a traveling show into villages for fifty miles around, to try to teach the villagers the value of sending their daughters to school. By now many Acholi parents have seen that educated girls can become nurses, teachers, or secretaries, and can earn a good livelihood. An increasing number are sending both sons and daughters to school, with the hard-working mothers especially making sacrifices to pay the school fees. It is most likely that in a few years the Acholi will have many women going on to the university colleges. I have the honor of being the first. Two others will be joining me at Makerere in the near future.

So it is that with the growing cash economy, the trend toward the town, and the spread of school education for both men and women, the horizons of Acholi children and young people, even in the villages, are gradually growing wider. Improved transportation facilities are being used by more and more people. Better roads are being built all over Uganda, some of them in Acholi going from village to village. Many families in once-remote village homes have their night's sleep interrupted, until they become used to the sound, by the constant line of huge lorries that go grinding up and down the slopes at night, taking produce to market. The whistle and rumble of trains breaks the silence in many places, since two years ago the railway line was extended across Acholi. From time to time an airplane will fly high over Acholi towns and villages. Then even the very young children may look up and, pointing to the moving object, merely remark, "Airplane, Mummy!" Swift and comfortable buses cover the distance between Acholi towns and Kampala in a matter of hours, a journey which in my own childhood took days.

The first time I travelled by bus, I remember, was in 1948, when I was seven years old. I cannot forget that first ride. I was travelling with my mother to my grandmother's house, about thirty-five miles away. I can still hear the noise of the engine and feel the bumping of the bus. It all seemed strange and frightening to me then, especially when I made a remarkable discovery. Wondering if we would ever get to Grandmother's house, I turned around to look at the passengers behind me. They were not moving at all. Everyone on the bus was sitting still, remaining in exactly the same position. When I looked out the window I saw that it was the trees and grass and houses along the road that were moving, not the people on the bus! To me this was an amazing sight. I was still wondering and trying to figure it all out when the bus stopped. "Come out, Apoko, come out!" my mother was saying. For we had reached my grandmother's home.

Again, some Acholi children come from rich families who, instead of using bicycles, own their own cars, thus making it possible for the families to do much more travelling. Motor cars from the towns and cities go whizzing by on the main roads, past the schools and homes and marketplaces, where children can always be found. Along these same roads, still, there will always be a stream of people walking, especially on market days. Men and boys can be seen with their bicycles, frequently carrying a friend or a wife or a child, and sometimes both, or a heavy load of produce, up hill and down. The women will be carrying headloads of firewood, perhaps, containers of water, or huge loads of market produce. Often they will have babies tied to their backs, sometimes with another child or two clinging to their skirts as the cars flash by.

Even an educated girl, like the one shown above, helps her mother with traditional chores. Below, young mothers learn new techniques of child care. (Photo above by Paul Almasy, courtesy World Health Organization, photo below courtesy UNESCO)

ACHOLI

● GULU

U G A N D A

KAMPALA ●

UGANDA

For the Acholi village men, except for the few like my father, who truly like to do farm work, are still prone to follow more leisurely pastimes—hunting, chatting in the market, attending funerals, drinking beer—leaving their women to carry the brunt of the heavy work. My Acholi classmate, a man, always argues with me about this. But I have observed too much of the respective responsibilities carried by the men and boys and the women and girls in my tribe, even nowadays, to feel that I can agree with him. Many times on market days, one will see adolescent girls carrying their headloads along the road, quite obviously annoyed by boys of their own age who may follow or taunt them. The marketplace is still a popular place for Acholi adolescents to make friends of the opposite sex.

Children and young people, at school and sometimes at home, are having more access to radio. The primary child who can still tell an Acholi folktale in dramatic detail, singing the songs in the story with gusto, also knows how to sing and twist to some of the current "pop songs." ... And even the youngest child, where there is a radio in the home, will want to twist to the song *Ye yekka Obote Waffe,* or "He alone, our Obote." (Dr. Obote is the President of Uganda.) Children also pick up stories from the radio, for Radio Uganda broadcasts children's programs in most Uganda languages now. The older children, along with their parents, often listen to the news.

Thus, with the increasing number of radios and even, as time goes on, television sets accessible to Acholi families and schools, it is likely that our children in the future will have better facilities for learning. Already they are becoming increasingly accustomed to modern changes and improve-

37

ments. More and more of them are learning many of the old tribal customs by word of mouth from their elders, not through experience, as we did. Often it seems to be only the oldest villagers who ponder and treasure the past. The children and youth are more apt to enjoy the modern and look to the future.

Song of Lawino: A Lament

by Okot p'Bitek

PART I

["Growing Up in Acholi" presented an inside view of traditional tribal life. We saw how the fixed roles of men and women were passed on through the training—the socializing—of young people. We saw the important part played by the tribe in this process. In short, we witnessed a society in the process of preserving its identity.

We also saw that certain changes are taking place in the traditional way of life. Girls are going to school, boys are leaving the village, men are earning money and not crops as payment, the number of cars and buses is increasing, and radios are becoming commonplace. These external changes have a jolting affect on the old way of doing things. As we have seen, social practices do not change easily, and, indeed, there may be good reasons why they should not change. But, whether or not social practices change, people are deeply affected by the transformation of their environments.

The poem you are about to read, "Song of Lawino," is a moving account of the effects of social change on people. A traditional Acholi wife, Lawino, tells how her husband, Ocol, complains because she "cannot dance the ballroom dance" or "use the primus stove" or "do my hair as white women do." She also tells of the

39

way she does these things—the way they have always been done
by Acholi women.

The author, Okot p'Bitek, is an Acholi. Born in northern
Uganda in 1931, he was educated in Uganda and later studied
education, law, and social anthropology in England. He has
lectured at Makerere University, Uganda, and played football
for the Uganda national team. Besides *Song of Lawino,* p'Bitek
has published a novel and several poems and articles. He trans-
lated *Song of Lawino* himself from the original Acholi.

As you read Part I, think of these questions:

What complaints does Ocol have about his wife, Lawino?

What complaints does she have about Ocol?

What do Lawino's words and images indicate about her way
of life?

What has Ocol lost through his modern education?]

. . . My husband pours scorn
On Black People,
He behaves like a hen
That eats its own eggs,
A hen that should be imprisoned under a basket. . . .

He says Black People are Primitive
And their ways are utterly harmful,
Their dances are mortal sins
They are ignorant, poor and diseased!

Ocol says he is a modern man,
A progressive and civilized man,
He says he has read extensively and widely
And he can no longer live with a thing like me

Who cannot distinguish between good and bad,
He says I am just a village woman,
I am of the old type,
And no longer attractive.

He says I am blocking his progress,
My head, he says,
Is as big as that of an elephant
But it is only bones,
There is no brain in it,
He says I am only wasting his time.

*   *   *

. . . Listen Ocol, my old friend,
The ways of your ancestors
Are good,
Their customs are solid
And not hollow,
They are not thin, not easily breakable,
They cannot be blown away
By the winds
Because their roots reach deep into the soil.

I do not understand
The ways of foreigners
But I do not despise their customs.
Why should you despise yours?

*   *   *

. . . When the drums are throbbing
And the black youths
Have raised much dust
You dance with vigor and health,
You dance naughtily with pride,

You dance with spirit,
You compete, you insult, you provoke,
You challenge all!
And the eyes of the young men become red!

Communal dancing can be found throughout Africa. These young dancers are Masai, from Kenya. (Photo from the film Munchhausen in Africa, *courtesy FPG, Inc.)*

The son of a man
And the daughter of a man
Shine forth in the arena.
Slave boys and girls
Dance differently from true-borns.

You dance with confidence
And you sing
Provocative songs,
Insulting and abusive songs,
Songs of praise,
Sad songs of broken loves,

42

Songs about shortage of cattle.
Most of the songs make someone angry.

*   *   *

It is true, Ocol,
I cannot dance the ballroom dance.
Being held so tightly
I feel ashamed,
Being held so tightly in public
I cannot do it,
It looks shameful to me!

They come to the dance dead drunk,
They drink white men's drinks
As well as *waragi.**
They close their eyes,
And they do not sing as they dance,
They dance silently like wizards.

*   *   *

If someone tries
To force me to dance this dance
I feel like hanging myself
Feet first!

I wish I could become
A meteorite
And I would know
Where to fall!

*   *   *

* A liquor distilled from bananas, resembling vodka or gin.

It is true
I cannot do my hair
As white women do.

Listen,
My father comes from Payira,
My mother is a woman of Koc!
I am a true Acholi,
I am not a half-caste,
I am not a slave girl;
My father was not brought home
By the spear,
My mother was not exchanged
For a basket of millet.

Ask me what beauty is
To the Acholi
And I will tell you;
I will show it to you
If you give me a chance!

You saw me once,
You saw my hair style
And you admired it,
And the boys loved it.
At the arena
Boys surrounded me
And fought for me.

My mother taught me
Acholi hair fashions;
Which fit the kind

44

Of hair of the Acholi,
And the occasion.

Listen,
Ostrich plumes differ
From chicken feathers,
A monkey's tail
Is different from that of the giraffe,
The crocodile's skin
Is not like the guinea fowl's,
And the hippo's is naked and hairless.

The hair of the Acholi
Is different from that of the Arabs;
The Indians' hair
Resembles the tail of the horse;
It is like sisal strings
And needs to be cut
With scissors.
It is black
And is different from that of white women.

A white woman's hair
Is soft like silk;
It is light
And brownish, like
That of the brown monkey,
And is very different from mine.
A black woman's hair
Is thick and curly. . . .

*   *   *

They cook their hair
With hot iron
And pull it hard
So that it may grow long.
Then they rope the hair
On wooden pens
Like a billy goat
Brought for the sacrifice
Struggling to free itself.

They fry their hair
In boiling oil
As if it were locusts,
And the hair sizzles,
It cries aloud in sharp pain
As it is pulled and stretched.
And the vigorous and healthy hair,
Curly, springy, and thick,
That glistens in the sunshine
Is left listless and dead
Like the elephant grass
Scorched brown by the fierce
February sun.
It lies lifeless
Like the sad and dying banana leaves
On a hot and windless afternoon.

*   *   *

Ocol, my friend,
Look at my skin,
It is smooth and black.
And my boyfriend

Who plays the *nanga**
Sings praises to it.

I am proud of the hair
With which I was born
And as no white woman
Wishes to do her hair
Like mine,
Because she is proud
Of the hair with which she was born,
I have no wish
To look like a white woman.

No leopard
Would change into a hyena,
And the crested crane
Would hate to be changed
Into the bald-headed,
Dung-eating vulture,
The long-necked and graceful giraffe
Cannot become a monkey.

*   *   *

My husband says
He rejects me
Because I do not appreciate
White men's foods,
And that I do not know
How to hold
The spoon and the fork.

* A harplike instrument.

He is angry with me
Because I do not know
How to cook
As white women do. . . .

He complains endlessly.
He says
Had I been to school
I would have learnt
How to use
White men's cooking stoves.

I confess,
I do not deny!
I do not know
How to cook like a white woman.

I cannot use the primus stove.
I do not know
How to light it,
And when it gets blocked
How can I prick it?
The thing roars
Like a male lion,
It frightens me!

They say
It once burst
And the flame burnt
A goat to death!

I really hate
The charcoal stove!

Your hand is always
Charcoal-dirty
And anything you touch
Is blackened;
And your fingernails
Resemble those of the poison woman.
It is so difficult to start.
You wait for the winds
To blow
But whenever you are in a hurry
The winds go off to visit
Their mothers-in-law. . . .

Traditional cooking and traditional roles. (Photo by Paul Almasy, courtesy UNICEF)

I am terribly afraid
Of the electric stove,

49

And I do not like using it
Because you stand up
When you cook.
Who ever cooked standing up? . . .

The white man's stoves
Are good for cooking
White men's food:
For cooking the tasteless,
Bloodless meat of cows
That were killed many years ago
And left in the ice
To rot!
For frying an egg
Which when ready
Is slimy like mucus,

For boiling hairy chicken
In saltless water.
You think you are chewing paper!
And the bones of the leg
Contain only clotted blood
And when you bite
The tip of the bones of the leg
It makes no cracking sound,
It tastes like earth!

The white man's stoves
Are for boiling cabbages
And for baking the light spongy thing
They call bread.

They are for warming up
Tinned beef, tinned fish,
Tinned frogs, tinned snakes,
Tinned peas, tinned beans,
Big broad beans
Tasteless like the *cooro*!*

They are for preparing
Foods for the toothless,
For infants and invalids,
It is for making tea or coffee!

You use the saucepan
And the frying pan
And other flat-bottomed things,
Because the stoves are flat
Like the face of the drum.

The earthen vegetable pot
Cannot sit on it,
There are no stones
On which to place
The pot for making millet bread.

Come, brother,
Come into my mother's house!
Pause a bit by the door,
Let me show you
My mother's house.

* A creeping plant whose tasteless fruit (beans) is used in children's games.

Look,
Straight before you
Is the central pole.
That shiny stool
At the foot of the pole
Is my father's revered stool.

Further on
The rows of pots
Placed one on top of the other
Are the stores
And cupboards.
Millet flour, dried carcasses
Of various animals,
Beans, peas,
Fish, dried cucumber . . .

Look up to the roof,
You see the hangings?
The string nets
Are called *cel.*
The beautiful long-necked jar
On your left
Is full of honey,
That earthen dish
Contains simsim paste;
And that grass pocket
Just above the fireplace
Contains dried white ants.

Here on your left
Are the grinding stones;

The big one
Ashen and dusty
And her daughter
Sitting in her belly
Are the destroyers of millet
Mixed with cassava
And sorghum.

The mother stone
Has a hollow stomach,
A strange woman
She never gets pregnant;
And her daughter
Never gets fatter
She gets smaller and smaller
Until she is finished. . . .

On this stone
They also grind
Dried beans and peas.
The sister stone,
The smaller one,
Clean and beautifully oiled
Like a girl
Ready for the *jok* dance,*
Is the simsim grinding stone.

And when my sister
Is grinding simsim
Mixed with groundnuts

* A religious ceremony.

And I am grinding
Millet mixed with sorghum
You hear the song of the stones,
You hear the song of the grains
And the seeds,
And above all these
The beautiful duet
By Lawino and her sister.

Oh, how I miss my sister
And how I miss the singing
While grinding millet in my mother's house!

*   *   *

In my mother's house
We eat sitting on the earth
And not on trees
Like monkeys;
The young men
Sit cross-legged
And a girl sits carefully
On one leg.
Father alone sits on the stool.
We all sit on skins
Or papyrus mats
On the earth.
The knives in my mother's house
Are for harvesting
Or for cutting up the meat
Before it is cooked:
But not for cutting millet bread.

We wash our hands clean
And attack the loaf
From all sides.
You mold a spoon
And dip it in the gravy
And eat it up

And you use your right hand
Even if you are left-handed:
This is good manners.
Only rude fellows
Use their left hands
For breaking millet bread.

I do not know
How to cook
Like white women;
I do not enjoy
White men's foods;
And how they eat—
How could I know?
And why should I know it?

White men's stoves
Are for cooking
White men's foods.
They are not suitable
For cooking
Acholi foods
And I am afraid of them. . . .

Song of Lawino: A Lament

PART II

[As we have seen in Part I of "Song of Lawino," one culture is neither better nor worse than any other culture—it is simply different. In fact, when we try to change a culture by importing aspects of another culture, disruption results. Notice what happens to Lawino. Not only is she asked to behave in ways that are foreign to her, but she is cut off from her husband's life. She is made to feel out of place.

Her husband, of course, suffers even greater humiliation because he has come to believe that his traditional ways are actually evil. He loses his pride, something Lawino never loses. This raises the question: which is more important, to become modern or to have dignity? All so-called developing countries face this question. The ideal answer, of course, is to have both: to take what is useful from other cultures and to keep what is most important in your own. But this is not always so easy.

In Part II of "Song of Lawino," we will learn more of the changes taking place in Africa as the result of Westernization. Many of these changes, of course, are beneficial and desired by Africans—for example, the introduction of modern medicine and technology. Some are perhaps less beneficial. But whether they are good or bad, all changes extract their human price.

56

As you read Part II, think of these questions:

How has the clock affected Ocol?

How does Lawino tell time?

What has happened to communication between Ocol and Lawino?]

My husband is angry
Because, he says,
I cannot keep time
And I do not know
How to count the years.

He asks me
How many days
There are in a year,
And how many weeks
In our moon.
But I cannot answer.
The number of moons
In nine weeks
I cannot say!
How can I tell?

Ocol has brought home
A large clock.
It goes tock-tock-tock-tock
And it rings a bell.

He winds it first
And then it goes!

57

But I have never touched it,
I am afraid of winding it!

I wonder what causes
The noise inside it!
And what makes it go! . . .

I do not know
How to tell the time
Because I cannot read
The figures.

To me the clock
Is a great source of pride
It is beautiful to see
And when visitors come
They are highly impressed!

And Ocol has strange ways
Of saying what the time is.
In the morning
When the sun is sweet to bask in
He says
"It is Eight o'clock!"
When the cock crows
For the first time
He says
"It is Five!"
Toward the middle of the night,
When wizards are getting ready,
Ocol says
"It is Eleven!"

And after sunset,
"It is Seven."

My head gets puzzled,
Things look upside-down
As if I have been
Turning round and round
And I am dizzy.

If my husband insists
What exact time
He should have morning tea
And breakfast,
When exactly to have coffee
And the exact time
For taking the family photograph—
Lunchtime, teatime,
And supper time—
I must first look at the sun,
The cock must crow
To remind me.

In our village
When someone is going
On a long journey,
When there is a hunt
Or communal hoeing,
People wake up early,
When the horizon in the East
Is aflame
And in the West
The Buffalo Star is ripe

Like a yellow and sweet mango
About to fall to the earth.

No one moves at midnight
Except wizards covered in ashes
Dancing stark naked
Armed with disemboweled frogs
And dead lizards.

Or young thieves
Looking for other men's daughters,
They travel fearless
Through the fiends
That sow smallpox
In the countryside.

They split the darkness
With their bare chests,
They smell out their loves
Through the thick dew!

When the sun has grown up
And the poisoned tips
Of its arrows painfully bite
The backs of the men hoeing
And of the women weeding or harvesting,
This is when
You take drinking water
To the workers.

Food is taken to the fields
When the men are exhausted.
They crack the bones of chicken

And eat much peas and beans
And heaps of millet bread
As big as elephant dung.

Then they return home
Leaving behind a large field
And houseflies
Fighting over bits of food
And excreta that were thrown away.

When the sun
Has cooled off,
The men and the youths
Visit the traps and pits,
They hunt edible rats,
Or hook fish
From the streams.

Others cut wooden dishes
Out of logs
Or make ropes for the cows
Or weave baskets
For the chicken house.
They repair the roofs
Of the granaries
Or make patterns on half-gourds.

You hear the flutes
Of the herdsmen
Bringing the cattle home.
The flute-songs mingle
With the lowing of the bulls.

*   *   *

Time has become
My husband's master,
It is my husband's husband.
My husband runs from place to place
Like a small boy,
He rushes without dignity.

And when visitors have arrived
My husband's face darkens,
He never asks you in,
And for greeting
He says
"What can I do for you?"

I do not know
How to keep the white man's time.
My mother taught me
The way of the Acholi
And nobody should
Shout at me
Because I know
The customs of our people!
When the baby cries
Let him suck milk
From the breast.
There is no fixed time
For breast feeding.

When the baby cries
It may be he is ill;
The first medicine for a child

Is the breast.
Give him milk
And he will stop crying,
And if he is ill
Let him suck the breast
While the medicine-man
Is being called
From the beer party.

Children in our homestead
Do not sleep at fixed times.
When sleep comes
Into their head
They sleep.
When sleep leaves their head
They wake up.

When a child is dirty
Give him a wash,
You do not first look at the sun!
When there is no water
In the house
You cannot wash the child
Even if it is time
For his bath!

Listen,
My husband,
In the wisdom of the Acholi
Time is not stupidly split up
Into seconds and minutes,

It does not flow
Like beer in a pot
That is sucked
Until it is finished.

It does not resemble
A loaf of millet bread
Surrounded by hungry youths
From a hunt.
It does not get finished
Like vegetables in the dish.

A lazy youth is rebuked,
A lazy girl is slapped,
A lazy wife is beaten,
A lazy man is laughed at,
Not because they waste time
But because they only destroy
And do not produce. . . .

Ocol laughs at me
Because, he says,
I do not know
The names of the moons,
That I do not know
How many moons in a year
And the number of Sabbaths
In one moon.

                      *   *   *

We all know the moon—
It elopes,

Climbs the hill
And falls down.

It lights up the night,
Youths like it,
Wizards hate it,
And hyenas howl
When the moon
Shines into their eyes. . . .

I do not know
The names of the moons
Because the Acholi
Do not name their moons.

During the *Ager* period*
Millet is sown,
Just before the rains
And as they sow
They raise much dust.

When the rains return
We say
The rains have fallen.
The period is called
Poto-kot.†
Then the millet seeds germinate.
Sometimes the rains come early,
Sometimes they return late.

* The end of the dry season, around the end of March.
† The start of the rainy season, in early April.

When the millet
Begins to flower
And the time
For the harvest is approaching
All the granaries are empty

An Acholi granary, open for airing. (Photo by Paula Foster)

And hunger begins
To bite people's tummies.
This period
Is called *Odunge,**
Because fierce hunger burns
People's insides
And they drink

* The weeding season, in May or June, when plants are still growing
and the reserve stock of food from the last harvest is running out;
hence this is a hungry period.

Vegetable soups
To deaden the teeth
Of the fire.

And as the millet
Begins to get ready for harvest,
Some women ask,
"Is this not my own garden?"
They take their harvest knives
And a small basket,
They cut one head here
And another one there,
And when someone laughs,
They ask,
"Whose garden have I spoiled?"
So the period
Just before the harvest
Is called
*Abalo-pa-nga.**

The Acoli know
The Wet Season
And the Dry Season.

Wet Season means
Hard work in the fields,
Sowing, weeding, harvesting.
It means waking up before dawn.

* Literally, "I have the right." This refers to a woman's right to cut her
crops before they are fully matured if severe hunger compells her to
do so. Others may accuse her of spoiling her garden, but she can
respond, "Abalo-pa-nga."

It means mud
And thick dew.
Herdboys dislike it,
Lazy people hate it.

Dry Season means pleasures,
It means dancing,
It means hunting
In freshly burnt plains.

You hear *otole** dance drums
And funeral songs.
You hear the horns and trumpets
And the moonlight dance songs
Floating in the air.

Youths in small groups
Go on the *apet*† hunting expeditions,
Great hunters stay alone
In the wilderness
Smoking the carcass of the cob
Or the buffalo.

Others go off to Pajule
To look for bridewealth,
For if you have no sister
Then kill an elephant.
You sell the teeth
And marry a wife,

* A traditional victory dance following a battle.
† An especially long journey made on foot across the plains, in search
  of antelope and cheetah.

Then you call your son
Ocan, because you are poor!

Dry Season means wooing
And eloping with girls,
It means the *moko** dance
When youths and girls
Get stuck to one another!

My husband says
My head is numb and empty
Because, he says,
I cannot tell
When our children were born.

I know that Okang,
My first-born,
Was born at the beginning
Of the Dry Season
And my little girl
In the middle of the rains.
Okang was born
In the middle of the famine
Called *Abongo-wang-dako.*†
They say
One night a man

---

* A mating dance performed only by young people who are eligible
for marriage.
† The name of a legendary famine. There is a well-known story of a
man who was so hungry during Abongo-wang-dako that he examined
his wife's eyes to see if she was asleep, because he wanted to sneak
into the kitchen for food. He became the laughing-stock of the village,
for no Acholi man is ever supposed to look into the kitchen.

69

Was so hungry
He got up
And felt his wife's eyes
To see if she was asleep
So that he might
Inspect the cooking pots.

And Atoo was born
After the smallpox fiends
Had just left the homestead.
The fiend found
Many people with bad hearts,
There was much quarrelling
And jealousy among women
And so many people perished.
I lost my father too,
That is why
The little girl was called Atoo.

A person's age
Is seen by looking at him or her.
A girl is grown up
When her breasts have come;
A young man's voice breaks
And hair appears
On his face
And below his belly button.

When a girl sees the moon
She is ripe,
After bearing three children
She begins to wither

And soon she becomes
A mother-in-law.
Then she is deeply respected.

A person's age
Is shown by what he or she does
It depends on what he or she is,
And on what kind of person
He or she is. . . .

African Child

by Camara Laye

PART I

[Tradition and change—the two main themes of this unit—can be found everywhere in Africa. Thus far we have focused mainly on one group of people, in East Africa. In "African Child" we cross the continent to Guinea, in West Africa.

Here again we find a head-on collision of tradition and modernization, but this time we see change in the making, so to speak. *Dark Child,* from which these selections are taken, is Camara Laye's autobiography. As the title suggests, it deals with his early years. Change, we are told, comes most easily to the young, but the following excerpts show that even the young can suffer the dilemma of old *versus* new.

Camara Laye, who was born in 1928, grew up in Guinea when it was still a French colony. His father was of the Malinke people, who founded the great Mali empire in the thirteenth century.

Camara Laye's natural ability and enterprise brought him success in the schools of the colony and finally a scholarship to study engineering in France. He stayed in Paris for six years, working for a while in an automobile factory. He wrote his autobiography during this time, to relieve his homesickness for Africa.

The book was first published in 1954 in France, where it was well received and in fact won a literary prize. Royalties from the sale of the book enabled Laye to return to Africa for a visit with his family and to continue his writing. Laye has also served as a member of the National Research Institute in Conakry (capital of the Republic of Guinea) and as a diplomat representing Guinea abroad.

As you read Part I, think of these questions:

What does the black snake represent in this story?

How does Camara Laye feel about this snake?

What conflicts does Camara Laye face?]

I was a little boy playing round my father's hut. How old would I have been at that time? I cannot remember exactly. I must have been very young; five, maybe six years old. My mother was in the workshop with my father, and I could just hear their familiar voices above the noise of the anvil and the conversation of the customers.

Suddenly I stopped playing, my whole attention fixed on a snake that was creeping round the hut. He really seemed to be "taking a turn" round the hut. After a moment I went over to him. I had taken in my hand a reed that was lying in the yard—there were always some lying around; they used to get broken off the fence of plaited reeds that marked the boundary of our compound—and I thrust this reed into the reptile's mouth. The snake did not try to get away: he was beginning to enjoy our little game; he was slowly swallowing the reed; he was devouring it, I thought, as if it were some delicious prey, drawing nearer to my hand. At last

73

the reed was almost entirely swallowed up, and the snake's jaws were terribly close to my fingers.

I was laughing. I had not the slightest fear, and now I know that the snake would have not hesitated much longer before burying his fangs in my fingers if, at that moment, Damany, one of the apprentices, had not come out of the workshop. The apprentice shouted to my father, and almost at once I felt myself lifted off my feet: I was safe in the arms of one of my father's friends!

There was a terrific commotion going on all round me; my mother shouting harder than anyone; and she gave me a few sharp slaps. I began to weep, more upset by the sudden uproar than by the blows I had received. A little later, mother solemnly warned me never to play such a game again; and I promised, although I could not really see where the danger in it lay.

My father's hut was near the workshop, and I would often play there beneath the veranda that ran round the outside. It was my father's private hut. It was built like all our huts, of mud that had been pounded and molded into bricks with water; it was round and proudly helmeted with thatch. It was entered by a rectangular doorway. Inside, a tiny window let in a thin shaft of daylight. On the right there was a bed, made of beaten earth like the bricks, spread with a simple wickerwork mat on which was a pillow stuffed with kapok. At the rear of the hut, right under the window where the light was strongest, were the toolboxes. On the left were the *boubous* [long, flowing gowns worn by women over their regular dresses] and the prayer-rugs. Finally, at the head of the bed, hanging over the pillow and watching my father's slumber, there was a series of pots that contained extracts from plants and the bark of trees. These pots all had metal

74

lids and they were profusely and curiously garlanded with chaplets of cowrie shells; it did not take me long to discover that they were the most important things in the hut; they contained the magic charms, those mysterious liquids that keep evil spirits at bay and, smeared on the body, make it invulnerable to black magic, to all kinds of black magic. My father, before he went to bed, never failed to smear his body with a little of each liquid, first one, then another, for each charm had its own particular property; but exactly *what* property I do not know: I left my father's house too soon.

*   *   *

Ever since that day I had been forbidden to play with snakes. I would run to my mother as soon as I saw one.

"There's a snake!" I would cry.

"What, another?" my mother would shout.

And she would come running out to see what sort of snake it was. If it was just a snake like any other snake—actually, they were all quite different!—she would beat it to death at once; and, like all the women of our country, she would work herself into a frenzy beating the snake to a pulp, whereas the men would content themselves with a single hard blow, neatly struck.

One day, however, I noticed a little black snake with a strikingly marked body that was proceeding leisurely in the direction of the workshop. I ran to warn my mother, as usual. But as soon as my mother saw the black snake, she said to me gravely:

"My son, this one must not be killed: he is not as other snakes, and he will not harm you; you must never interfere with him."

Everyone in our compound knew that this snake must not

be killed; excepting myself, and, I suppose, my little play-mates, who were just ignorant children.

"This snake," my mother added, "is your father's guiding spirit."

I gazed dumbfounded at the little snake. He was proceeding calmly toward the workshop; he was moving gracefully, very sure of himself, and almost as if conscious of his immunity; his body, black and brilliant, glittered in the harsh light of the sun. When he reached the workshop, I noticed for the first time, cut out level with the ground, a small hole in the wall. The snake disappeared through this hole.

"Look," said my mother, "the serpent is going to pay your father a visit."

Although I was familiar with the supernatural, this sight filled me with such astonishment that I was struck dumb. What business would a snake have with my father? And why this particular snake? No one had to kill him, because he was my father's guiding spirit! At any rate, that was the explanation my mother had given me. But what exactly *was* a "guiding spirit"? What were these guiding spirits that I found everywhere, forbidding one thing, commanding another to be done? I could not understand it at all, though their presences were around me as I grew to manhood. There were good spirits, and there were evil ones; and more evil than good ones, it seemed to me. And how was I to know that this snake was harmless? It looked the same as any other snake; it was, of course, a *black* snake, and certainly there was something unusual about it; but, after all, it *was* only a snake! I was absolutely baffled, but I did not ask my mother about it: I felt I would have to ask my father about it, almost as if this mystery was something in which women could have no part; it was a mysterious affair that could be discussed only with men. I decided to wait until nightfall.

Immediately after the evening meal, when the palavers were over, my father bade his friends farewell and went to sit under the veranda of his hut; I went and sat near him. I began by questioning him in a roundabout manner, as all children do, and on every subject under the sun. Finally, unable to restrain myself any longer, I asked:

"My father, what is that little snake that comes to visit you?"

"What snake do you mean?"

"Why, the little black snake that my mother forbids us to kill."

"Ah!" he said.

He gazed at me for a long while. He seemed to be considering whether to answer or not. Perhaps he was thinking about how old I was, perhaps he was wondering if it was not a little too soon to confide such a secret to a twelve-year-old boy. Then suddenly he made up his mind.

"That snake," he said, "is the guiding spirit of our race. Can you understand that?"

"Yes," I answered, although I did not understand very well.

"That snake," he went on, "has always been with us; he has always made himself known to one of us. In our time, it is to me that he has made himself known."

"That is true," I said.

And I said it with all my heart, for it seemed obvious to me that the snake could have made himself known to no one but my father. Was not my father the head man in our compound? Was it not my father who had authority over all the blacksmiths in our district? Was he not the most skilled? Was he not, after all, my father?

"How did he make himself known?" I asked.

"First of all, he made himself known in the semblance of a dream. He appeared to me several times in slumber, and he told me the day on which he would appear to me in reality: he gave me the precise time and place. But when I really saw him for the first time, I was filled with fear. I took him for a snake like any other snake, and I had to keep myself in control or I would have tried to kill him. When he saw that I did not receive him kindly, he turned away and departed the way he had come. And there I stood, watching his depart, and wondering all the time if I should not simply have killed him then and there; but a power greater than myself stayed my hand and prevented me from pursuing him. I stood watching him disappear. And even then, at that very moment, I could easily have overtaken him; a few strides would have been enough; but I was struck motionless by a kind of paralysis. Such was my first encounter with the little black snake."

He was silent a moment, then went on:

"The following night, I saw the snake again in my dream. 'I came as foretold,' he said, 'but thou didst not receive me kindly; nay, rather did I perceive that thou didst intend to receive me unkindly: I did read it thus in thine eyes. Wherefore dost thou reject me? Lo, I am the guiding spirit of thy race, and it is even as the guiding spirit of thy race that I make myself known to thee, as the most worthy. Therefore, forbear to look with fear upon me, and beware that thou dost not reject me, for behold, I bring thee good fortune.' After that, I received the serpent kindly when he made himself known to me a second time; I received him without fear, I received him with loving kindness, and he has brought me nothing but good."

78

My father again was silent for a moment, then he said:

"You can see for yourself that I am not more gifted than any other man, and even that I have less than others, since I give everything away, and would even give away the last thing I had, the shirt on my back. Nevertheless, I am better known than other men, and my name is on everyone's tongue, and it is I who have authority over all the black-smiths in the five cantons. If these things are so, it is by virtue of the snake alone, who is the guiding spirit of our race. It is to this snake that I owe everything, and it is he likewise who gives me warning of all that is to happen. Thus, I am never surprised, when I awake, to see this or that person wait-ing for me outside my shop: I already know that he or she will be there. No more am I surprised when this or that motor bicycle or bicycle breaks down, or when an accident happens to a clock: because I had foreknowledge of what would come to pass. Everything is transmitted to me in the course of the night, together with an account of all the work I shall have to perform, so that from the start, without hav-ing to cast about in my mind, I know how to repair whatever is brought to me; and it is these things that have established my renown as a craftsman. I owe it to the guiding spirit of our race."

He was silent; and then I understood why, when my father used to come back from a walk, he could enter the workshop and say to the apprentices: "During my absence, this or that person has been here, he was dressed in such and such a way, he came from such and such a place and brought with him such and such a piece of work to be done." And all marvelled at this curious knowledge. Now I understood how my father obtained his information. When I raised my eyes, I saw that my father was watching me.

"I have told you all these things, little one, because you are my son, the eldest of my sons, and because I have nothing to hide from you. There is a certain form of behavior to observe, and certain ways of acting in order that the guiding spirit of our race may approach you also. I, your father, was observing that form of behavior which persuades our guid-

In Africa the snake symbolizes the forces of nature, with which men communicate. In the West, however, the snake has come to symbolize evil, as in the Garden of Eden. Such differences in culture lead to conflict for those educated in two traditions. (Photo by Charles Uht, courtesy The Museum of Primitive Art)

ing spirit to visit us. Oh, perhaps not consciously. But nevertheless, it is true that if you desire the guiding spirit of our race to visit you one day, if you desire to inherit it in your turn, you will have to conduct yourself in the selfsame manner; from now on it will be necessary for you to be more and more in my company."

He gazed at me with burning eyes, then suddenly he heaved a sigh.

"I fear, I very much fear, little one, that you are not often enough in my company. You are all day at school, and one day you shall depart from that school for a greater one. You will leave me, little one. . ."

And again he heaved a sigh. I saw that his heart was heavy within him. The hurricane-lamp hanging on the veranda cast a harsh glare on his face. He suddenly seemed to me like an old man.

"Father!" I cried.

"Son . . . ," he whispered.

And I was no longer sure whether I ought to continue to attend the school or whether I ought to remain in the workshop: I felt unutterably confused.

"Go now," said my father.

I got up and went to my mother's hut. The night was full of sparkling stars; an owl was hooting nearby. Ah, what was the right path for me? Did I know yet where the path lay? My perplexity was boundless as the sky, and mine was a sky, alas, without any stars. . . . I entered my mother's hut, which at that time was mine also, and went to bed at once. But sleep evaded me, and I tossed restlessly on my bed.

"What's the matter with you?" asked my mother.

"Nothing."

No, I couldn't find anything to say.

"Why don't you go to sleep?" went on my mother.

"I don't know."

"Go to sleep!" she said.

"Yes," I said.

"Sleep. . . . Nothing can resist sleep," she said sadly.

Why did she, too, appear so sad? Had she divined my distress? Anything that concerned me she sensed very deeply. I was trying to sleep, but I shut my eyes and lay still in vain;

the image of my father under the storm-lantern would not leave me. He had suddenly seemed so old, he who was so youthful, so active, more youthful and more active than any of us, and who in the running of races never let himself be outstripped by anyone, whose limbs were swifter than the limbs of all our young men. . . . "Father! . . . Father!" I kept repeating it. "Father, what must I do, what is the right thing to do?" And I wept quietly and, weeping, fell asleep.

After that, we never mentioned the little black snake again: my father had spoken to me about him for the first and the last time. But from that time forth, as soon as I saw the little snake, I would run and sit in the workshop, I would watch him glide through the little hole in the wall. As if informed of his presence . . . my father would stroke him with his hand, and the snake would accept the caress with a quivering of his whole body: never did I see the little snake attempt to do the slightest harm to my father. That caress and the answering tremor—but I ought to say: that appealing caress and the answering tremor—threw me each time into an inexpressible confusion: I would imagine I know not what mysterious conversation . . . the hand inquired and the tremor replied. . . .

Yes, it was like a conversation. Would I, too, converse like that one day? No; I was still attending the school. Yet I should have liked so much to place my hand, my own hand, on the snake, and to understand and listen to that tremor, too; but I did not know how the snake would have taken my hand, and I felt now that he would have nothing to tell me; I was afraid that he would never have anything to tell me. . . .

Contemporary African women still use traditional markets as above, but today they also have the choice of shopping in a modern store, like the one shown below. (Photos by Paul Almasy, courtesy World Health Organization)

Old and New—African boys use a modern tape recorder to capture and preserve the sounds of a traditional musician. (Photo by Paul Almasy, courtesy UNESCO)

African Child

[As Camara Laye grew older (and therefore spent more years in school), he developed more modern tastes. As would be expected, the nontraditional aspects of his education led him further and further away from his father's way of life.

When he reached his teens, he was sent away to boarding school in Conakry. This was the fashionable thing to do among progressive families, because such schools provided the most modern (i.e., Western) education. On holidays he would return home to Kouroussa, and "Each time . . . I would find my hut newly decorated with white clay; my mother would be all impatience to show me the improvements which she had made in it from year to year."

Why did his mother modernize his hut? Was it because she wanted him to change? Or was it because she wanted to "doctor up" the old ways so that he wouldn't want to leave them altogether?

The answers to these questions are not clear-cut; human emotions are not simple. But whether parents actually encourage their children to change or simply allow change to take place, they are instrumental in their children's development. If nothing else, they provide the opportunity for their offspring to have new and different experiences. The result is not always comfortable, for children or parents.

As you read Part II, think of these questions:

What conflicts does Camara Laye experience? What conflicts does his mother experience?

Why is Camara Laye's mother opposed to his going to France?

How does Camara Laye feel about going to France?]

At first, my hut was just like any other. And then, gradually, it had begun to take on a more and more Europeanized appearance. I say "had begun to," for the resemblance always remained partial, though I was very conscious of it; not merely because of the additional comfort it offered, but because it was the living proof, the tangible proof, of the great love my mother felt for me. Yes, I used to pass most of the year at Conakry, but I was still her favorite son: I could see that easily. And I did not even need to see it: I knew it. But in the appearance of the hut I could see it as well as feel it.

"Well, what do you think of it?" my mother would ask.

"It's wonderful," I would reply.

And I would give her a great hug: that was all the thanks my mother expected. But it was indeed "wonderful," and I did not suspect how much ingenuity had gone into it, how much trouble my mother had taken in order to create—from the simplest materials—those modest equivalents of European mechanical appliances.

The main article of furniture, the one which immediately caught the eye, was the divan bed. At first it had been just like the bed in her own hut, a bed like any other bed in our country, a bed made of clay bricks. Then the central bricks had been removed, leaving only two supports, one at the foot and one at the head; and planks had taken the place of the bricks. On this improvised bedstead—crude but not uncomfortable—my mother finally placed a mattress stuffed with rice straw. Thus it became a comfortable and fairly spacious bed, big enough for three or even four.

But it was hardly spacious enough to accommodate all the friends, the innumerable friends, both boys and girls, who would come and visit me on certain evenings. I cannot remember just how, piled all together on the bed, we managed to find room to strum a guitar, nor yet how my friends got air enough for singing.

I do not know whether my mother cared very much for these meetings, but she put up with them, comforting herself probably with the thought that at least I was in my own compound, not hanging around Lord knows where. As for my father, he thought it was quite in order. As I scarcely saw him during the day, busy as I was visiting this or that friend's house (if I had not gone off on some more extensive trip), he would come and knock on my door, I would cry: "Come in!" and he would enter, saying "Good evening" to everyone, and would ask me how I had spent my day. After a few more words, he would go away. He understood that, although his presence was welcome—and it really was—it was at the same time very intimidating to such a youthful and lively gathering as ours.

My mother's attitude was completely different. Her hut was next to mine, and their doors faced each other: my mother had only to take a single step and she was inside my hut. She used to do so without any warning; she never

85

knocked at the door, she just walked straight in. Suddenly, there she would be standing before us, without the slightest sound from the door; she would look very closely at everyone before saying good evening.

Oh! it was not the faces of my men friends that she scrutinized; they were my own affair; they did not matter. No, it was the girls' faces that my mother used to inspect; and she very soon picked out the faces she did not like. I must admit that in these gatherings there were sometimes young women of rather loose habits, and whose reputation was a little tarnished. But how could I forbid them to come? Did I even want to do so? If they were a little more worldly-wise than was necessary, they were also generally the most amusing. But my mother thought otherwise, and she never used to beat about the bush.

"You," she would say, "what are you doing her? Your place is not with my son. Go back home. If I see you here again, I'll have something to tell your mother about you. I warn you."

If the girl did not make off fast enough, or if she did not extract herself quickly enough from the jumble on the divan, my mother would pull her out by the arm and thrust her toward the open door.

"Go on," she would cry, "get back home."

And with her hands she would pretend to be chasing away some too adventurous fowl. Only then would she say good evening to everyone.

I did not care much for this procedure. I did not care for it at all. Reports of the insults were spread abroad; and whenever I invited a girlfriend to come and visit me, she would say as often as not:

"And what if your mother catches me?"

"She won't eat you."

"No, but she'll start shouting and show me the door."

And I would stand there in front of the girl, wondering: "Is there really any reason why my mother should turn her out of doors?" And I did not always know. I used to live in Conakry for the greater part of the year, and I did not know all the details of Kouroussa gossip. But I could hardly say to the girl: "Have people been talking about you? And if you've had any affairs, do you think my mother knows about them?" It exasperated me.

As I grew older I became more passionate; I no longer had merely half-hearted friendships or even love affairs. I did not have only Marie or Fanta—although at first it was Marie and Fanta I had as friends. But Marie was on holiday at Bela, at her father's; and Fanta was my "regular" girl. I respected her; and even if I had wanted to go further (and I did not want to), custom would have forbidden it. The rest . . . the rest were unimportant, but they existed nevertheless. Could my mother fail to understand the growing ardor of my blood?

She understood it only too well. Often she would get up in the middle of the night and come and make sure that I was alone in bed. She would generally make her rounds toward midnight, striking a match to light my bed. If I happened to be awake, I would pretend to be asleep; then, as if the lighted match had disturbed me, I would pretend to wake with a start.

"What's the matter?" I would cry.

"Are you asleep?" my mother would ask.

"Yes, I was asleep. Why did you wake me up?"

"Good, go to sleep again."

"But how can I sleep if you keep waking me up?"

"Don't get worked up," she would say. "Go to sleep."

But I did not care much for this kind of treatment. And I used to complain about it to Kouyaté and Check Omar, who at that time were my most intimate friends.

"Am I not old enough to look after myself?" I would ask. "I was considered sufficiently grown up to be given my own hut; but how can I call my hut my own if people can enter it at any hour of the day or night?"

"It shows that your mother loves you very much," they would answer. "You are not going to complain of that?"

"No," was all I could say.

But I could not help thinking that her affection for me might have been a little less exclusive and less tyrannical. And it was obvious that Check and Kouyaté enjoyed more freedom than I was allowed.

"Don't brood over it so," Kouyaté would say. "Play us your guitar."

I would go and take down my guitar—Kouyaté had taught me to play. In the evening, instead of staying in my hut, we would go strolling through the streets of the town, Kouyaté and I, strumming on our guitars, while Check played the banjo and we all three sang in harmony. Girls who often were already in bed when we passed their compound would wake up and listen to us. Those who were friends of ours would recognize our voices; they would get up, dress hastily, and run to join us. Though only three of us had started out, soon we would be six, and ten, and sometimes even fifteen, all of us rousing the echoes in the sleeping streets.

Kouyaté and Check had been my school-fellows in the primary school at Kouroussa. They were both quick witted and particularly gifted at mathematics. I can still remember how, when the master had barely finished dictating a problem, they would both of them jump up and take him the finished sum. This amazing rapidity used to fill us all with wonder, but also used to fill me with discouragement, even though I always used to get my own back in French. But from that time onward—despite—or perhaps because of this competitive spirit—we had been friends: but it was a friendship such as only very young schoolboys know—not very well founded, and impermament.

Our real friendship did not begin until after I had left our home town, in fact, to study in Conakry, and Kouyaté and Check had left to continue their studies at, respectively, the high schools of Popoda and Dakar. We exchanged numerous and very lengthy letters, in which we used to describe our life at school and compare notes on our lessons. Then when the holidays came we met again in Kouroussa, and we soon became inseparable.

At first our parents had not looked upon our friendship with any great favor. Either we used to disappear for whole days, forgetting mealtimes and the meals themselves, or else we used to stay in the compound, so that at mealtimes there would be two unexpected guests. Such behavior was undoubtedly a little free and easy. But this disfavor did not last long. Our parents soon realized that if we disappeared for two out of every three days, the two guests would put in an appearance only on every third day; and they soon accepted the very fair and judicious rotation we had put into practice without consulting them.

"But couldn't you have told me?" my mother used to say. "Couldn't you have given me notice, so that I could have prepared something special?"

"No," I would reply. "Our sole wish was that no one

should make any special preparation for us. All we wanted
was the usual daily meal."

*   *   *

When I went back to Kouroussa with my proficiency cer-
tificate in my pocket, and feeling, I must confess, a little
swollen-headed by my success, I was of course received with
open arms, just as I had been received at the end of every
scholastic year, with the same eagerness, the same warm affection. This year, a fresh sense of pride was there. On the
road from the station to our compound, there had been the
most enthusiastic demonstrations to welcome me, and they
had all sprung from the same love, the same friendship. But
even as my parents pressed me to their breasts, my mother
rejoicing more at my return than at the diploma I had won,
my mind was uneasy, especially as regards my mother.

*Camara Laye's early education took place in a classroom similar to this
one, in Nairobi, Kenya. (Photo by George Holton, courtesy UNICEF)*

This was because before leaving Conakry the head of the school had sent for me and had asked me if I would like to go to France to complete my studies. I had blithely answered "Yes," but I had said it without consulting my parents, without having consulted my mother. My uncles in Conakry had told me that it was a unique opportunity, and that I did not deserve to live if I turned it down. What would my parents say, particularly my mother? I did not feel at all comfortable, I waited until the ecstatic greetings had died down a little and then I exclaimed, as if the news would be a source of delight to everyone:

"And that's not all; the headmaster wants to send me to France!"

"To France?" said my mother.

I saw her face contract.

"Yes, I shall be given a scholarship. It will not cost you anything."

"As if the cost mattered," said my mother. "Do you mean to say you're going to leave us again?"

"Well, I don't know yet."

I could see what I had already feared, that I had been hasty and too imprudent in saying "Yes" to the headmaster.

"You're not going," said my mother.

"No," I said, "but it would not be for longer than a year."

"A year?" said my father. "A year, that's not so long."

"What?" my mother broke in sharply. "A year isn't so very long? For the last four years our son has hardly ever been with us, except for the holidays, and you can stand there and say a year is not so very long?"

"Oh, well . . . ," my father began.

"No, no," my mother cried, "our son is not going. Let that be the end of the matter."

91

"All right," said my father, "we won't mention it again. For this is the day of his return, the day of his success. Let us rejoice. We'll talk about the other thing later on."

We said no more about it, for people were beginning to crowd into the compound, eager to celebrate my return.

Late that night, when everyone was in bed, I went and sat beside my father on the veranda of his hut. The headmaster had said that he required my father's official consent before he could do anything, and that this consent should reach him with the shortest delay.

"My father," I said, "when the headmaster asked me if I would like to go to France, I said, 'Yes.' "

"Ah! You've already accepted?"

"I couldn't help saying 'Yes.' I didn't think what I was saying at the time, or what you and my mother would think."

"Do you really want to go there?" he asked.

"Yes," I said. "My Uncle Marmadou told me that it was a unique opportunity."

"You could have gone to Dakar. Your Uncle Marmadou went to Dakar."

"It wouldn't be the same thing."

"No, it would not be the same thing. But how are we going to break it to your mother?"

"Then do you agree to my departure?" I cried.

"Yes. . . . Yes, I'm willing. Because of you. But do you hear, it's because of you I'm doing it, for your own good."

And he was silent awhile.

"You see," he said, "it's something I've often thought about. I've thought about it in the silence of the night and in the clangor of the forge. I knew quite well that one day you would leave us. I knew it the very first day you set foot in school. I watched you studying with such eagerness, such passionate eagerness! . . . Yes, since that day, I knew how it would be; and gradually I resigned myself to it."

"Father!" I said.

"Each one follows his own destiny, my son. Men can do nothing to change it. The opportunity is within your reach: you must seize it. You've already seized one, seize this one, too; make sure of it. There are still so many things to be done in our land. . . . Yes, I want you to go to France; I want that now just as much as you do. Soon we'll be needing men here like you. . . . Maybe you'll not be gone too long!"

We sat for a long time without saying anything under the veranda, looking into the night. Then suddenly my father said in a broken voice:

"Promise me that you will come back?"

"I shall come back," I said.

"These distant lands . . . ," he whispered slowly.

He left the phrase unfinished: he went on looking out into the darkness. I could see him, by the light of the storm-lantern, looking out into the night as if at a fixed point, and frowning as if he was uneasy or dissatisfied at what he saw there.

"What are you looking at?" I asked.

"Beware of ever deceiving anyone," he said. "Be upright in thought and deed. And God shall be with you."

Then he made what seemed a gesture of despair and turned his eyes away from the darkness.

The next day, I wrote to the headmaster that my father had given his permission. And I kept it a secret from everyone; I confided only in Kouyaté. Then, I began travelling round the district. I could go anywhere I liked; I visited the nearby towns; I went to Kankan, which is our holy city. When I came back, my father showed me the letter which

93

the headmaster of the Technical College had sent him. The headmaster confirmed my departure and named the French school where I was to study: the school was at Argenteuil.

"Do you know where Argenteuil is?" asked my father.

"No," I said. "I'll go and have a look."

I went and looked it up in my dictionary and I saw that Argenteuil was only a few miles from Paris.

"It's near Paris," I said.

And I began dreaming about Paris! Then my thoughts returned suddenly to my mother.

"Have you told my mother yet?" I asked.

"No," he replied. "We'll go together and give her the news."

"You wouldn't like to tell her yourself?"

"By myself? No, my son. Believe me, even if both of us go, we'll be outnumbered."

And we went to look for my mother. We found her crushing millet for the evening meal. My father stood a long while watching the pestle rising and falling in the mortar. He hardly knew where to begin. He knew that the decision he had to make would hurt my mother, and he himself had a heavy heart. He stood there watching the pestle and saying nothing; and I dared not lift my eyes. But my mother did not take long to guess what was in the wind. She only had to look at us in order to understand everything, or almost everything.

"What do you want?" she said. "Can't you see I'm busy?"

And she began pounding faster and faster.

"Don't go so fast," my father said, "you'll wear yourself out."

"Are you trying to teach me how to pound millet?" she said.

94

And then all of a sudden she went on angrily:

"If you want to discuss our son's departure for France, you can save your breath. He's not going."

"That's just it," said my father, "you don't know what you're talking about. You do not realize what such an opportunity means to him."

"And I don't want to know," she said.

Suddenly she dropped the pestle and took a few steps toward us.

"Shall I never have peace of mind?" she cried. "Yesterday it was the school at Conakry; today it's a school in France; tomorrow . . . what will it be next? Every day there's some mad scheme to take my son away from me! . . . Have you already forgotten how sick he was at Conakry? But that's not enough for you: now you want to send him to France! Are you crazy? Or do you want to send me out of my mind? I'll certainly end up raving mad. . . . 'And as for you," she cried, turning toward me, "you are nothing but an ungrateful son. Any excuse is good enough for you to run away from your mother. But this time it won't be as you want: you'll stop right here. Your place is here. What are they thinking about, at the school? Do they imagine I am going to live my whole life apart from my son? Die with him far away? Have they no mothers, those people? But they can't have mothers, of course. They would not have gone so far away from home if they'd had mothers."

And she lifted her eyes to the sky and addressed the heavens:

"He's been away from me so many years already!" she said. "And now they want to take him away to their own land! . . ."

Then she lowered her gaze and looked at my father again.

"Would you let them do that? Have you no heart?"

"Woman! Woman!" said my father. "Don't you know it's for his own good?"

"His own good? The best thing for him is to stay here with us. Hasn't he learned enough already?"

"Mother," I began.

But she turned on me violently.

"You be quiet. You're still just a little boy, a nobody. What do you want to go away for? Do you so much as know how people live out there? . . . No, you don't know anything about it. And tell me this, who's going to look after you? Who's going to mend your clothes? Who'll cook for you?"

"Come, come," said my father, "be reasonable. The white men don't die of hunger."

"So you haven't realized, you poor crazy thing! You haven't noticed that they don't eat as we do! This child will fall sick; that's what will happen. And then what will I do? What will become of me? Oh, once I had a son, but now I have a son no more!"

I went up to her and pressed her to me.

"Get away from me," she shouted. "You're no son of mine."

But she did not push me away; she was weeping and she held me closely to her.

"You won't leave me alone, will you? Tell me you won't leave me alone."

But now she knew that I would go away and that she could not stop my departure, that nothing could stop it. Perhaps she had known that from the first. Yes, she must have guessed at the workings of the inner wheels which, from the school in Kouroussa, led me to Conakry and

96

would finally take me to France; and all the time she had been talking and fighting against it, she must have been watching the wheels going round and round: first this wheel, then that one, and then this third and greater wheel, then still more wheels, many more wheels perhaps, that no one else could see. And how could their working be stopped? We could only watch them turning and turning, watch the wheels of destiny turning and turning: my destiny was to go away from home. And my mother began to direct her anger against those who, to her mind, were taking me away from her once again. But already they were only useless shreds of anger.

"Those people are never satisfied," she said. "They want to have everything. As soon as they set eyes on a thing, they want it for themselves."

"You must not malign them," I replied.

"No," she said bitterly, "I shall not malign them."

And finally she found that her anger and her rage were spent. She laid her head on my shoulder and wept noisily. My father had crept away. And I held her close. I dried her tears, I said . . . what did I say to her?

Everything and anything that came into my head, but nothing was of any importance. I don't think my mother understood a word of what I was saying; all she was aware of was the sound of my voice. And that was enough. Her sobs gradually grew quieter, and less frequent. . . .

That was how my departure was arranged. And so one day I stepped on a plane for France. Oh! it was a terrible parting! I do not like to think of it. I can still hear my mother wailing; I still can see my father, unable to hide his tears; I can still see my sisters, my brothers. . . . No, I do not like to remember that parting. It was as if I was being torn apart.

In Conakry, the headmaster told me that the plane would land at Orly.

"From Orly," he said, "you will be taken to Paris, to the Invalides station. There you will take the Metro [subway] to St. Lazare station, where you will find the train for Argenteuil."

He unfolded a Metro map and showed me the route I would be taking in the depths of the earth. But the map meant nothing to me, and the very idea of travelling underground was extremely vague to me.

"Are you sure you understand?" the headmaster asked me.

"Yes," I said.

But I did not quite understand everything.

"Take the map with you."

I slipped it into my pocket. The headmaster looked at me.

"You're not overdressed," he said.

I was wearing white cotton trousers and an open-necked sportshirt, sleeveless; on my feet I was wearing sandals and white socks.

"You'll have to wear more over there. At this time of the year it's already beginning to get colder."

I left for the airport with Marie and my uncles; Marie was going with me as far as Dakar, where she was to continue her studies. Marie. . . . I got into the plane with her. I was crying; we were all crying. Then the propeller began to turn. In the distance, my uncles were waving to us for the last time. And the earth, the land of Guinea, began to drop rapidly away.

"Are you glad to be going?" Marie asked me when the plane was nearing Dakar.

"I don't know," I answered. "I don't think so."

And when the plane landed at Dakar, Marie said to me: "Will you be coming back?"

Her face was wet with tears.

"Yes," I said, "yes. . . ."

And nodded in the affirmative again as if I fell back, right back in my seat, for I did not want anyone to see my tears. Surely I would be coming back! I sat for a long while without moving, my arms folded, tightly folded, to stifle the heaving of my breast.

Later on, I felt something hard when I put my hand in my pocket. It was the map of the Metro. . . .

Three Poems

[People need a means to express their feelings. Poetry has always been one of these means. In fact, it is the oldest and most traditional form of human expression; the most profound feelings of all ages and cultures have been recorded in poetry. It is no surprise, then, that much of the poetry of modern Africa deals with the emotional turmoil of change.

All three poems you are about to read were published within the past ten years, one as recently as 1967, and all three were written by Africans.

Kwesi Brew, the author of "Ancestral Faces," was born in 1928 at Cape Coast, Ghana, and studied at the University College, Accra. He entered the Public Service in 1953 and is currently Ghana's Ambassador to Senegal.

Ismael Hurreh, the author of "Pardon Me," was born in Somalia in 1940 and attended the University of New Mexico. After teaching secondary school in Africa, he returned to the United States to study at Syracuse University, where he was in 1967, when this poem appeared.

Leopold Sedar Senghor, the author of "Totem," is one of the most famous writers and statesmen of modern Africa. Born in 1906, since 1960 he has been the President of Senegal and is universally known as the major spokesman for "negritude."

As you read these poems, think of what you have been learning about Africa. What do these poems say about tradition? What do they say about change? What do they say about all societies?

A hundred or two hundred years from now, when historians look back at Africa in the 1960's, they will study the economics, politics, and society of the times. But when all their evidence is run through the supercomputers, if they still want to know how the people felt about their lives, they will have to turn to art and literature. That is what we are doing now.

As you read each poem, think of these questions:

What is the theme of the poem?

How does it relate to tradition and change?

How does it compare with the themes of the other poems?]

Ancestral Faces

by Kwesi Brew

They sneaked into the limbo of time
But could not muffle the gay jingling
Bells on the frothy necks
Of the sacrificial sheep that limped and nodded
    after them;
They could not hide the moss on the bald pate
Of their reverent heads;
And the gnarled barks of the wawa trees;*
Nor the rust on the ancient state-swords;
Nor the skulls studded with grinning cowries;†
They could not silence the drums,
The fibre of their souls and ours—
The drums that whisper to us behind black sinewy
    hands.
They gazed.
And sweeping like white locusts through the
    forests

---

* Wawa trees are known for their hardness and resistance to insects
and disease.
† Cowries are shells formerly used as money in West Africa.

Saw the same men, slightly wizened,
Shuffle their sandalled feet to the same rhythm.
They heard the same words of wisdom uttered
Between puffs of pale blue smoke:
They saw us,
And said: They have not changed!

The importance of ancestors in traditional life is the theme of much African art. These carvings show the Senufo tribe of the Ivory Coast. (Photo by Elisabeth Little)

Pardon Me

by Ismael Hurreh

pardon me father if I am a disappointment to what you
expected of me
                              pardon me father
if I cannot slaughter other tribesmen
if I do not say my prayers in the morning
if I turn my back on some of your advice
                              because father
although your blood runs in my veins
although I too have been a nomad
although I've slept under roofless huts
                              eyeing the moon
and raising my hands to God
and envying His might
time has unfolded many strange sheets
and spread them between us
time has uprooted me
time has transplanted me to grounds
where prayer is of no use,

and mother pardon me for digging your bones out
(your bones that were buried here)

> pardon me

if I had forgotten that you were buried here.

Totem

by Léopold Sédar Senghor

I must hide him in my innermost veins
The Ancestor whose stormy hide is shot with lightening
    and thunder
My animal protector, I must hide him
That I may not break the barriers of scandal:
He is my faithful blood that demands fidelity
Protecting my naked pride against
Myself and the scorn of luckier races.